Courage to Thrive

TRIUMPH IN THE FACE OF ADVERSITY

Dr. Stephen Trudeau

Royce Publishing
Los Angeles, California

Copyright © 2015 Stephen Trudeau Psy.D.

All rights reserved. No part of this publication may be reproduced, distributed or transmitted in any form or by any means, including photocopying, recording, or other electronic or mechanical methods, without the prior written permission of the publisher, except in the case of brief quotations embodied in critical reviews and certain other noncommercial uses permitted by copyright law. This book may be purchased for educational, business, or sales promotional use. Quantity sales, please contact the address below.

Publisher's Note

This publication is designed to provide accurate and authoritative information in regard to the subject matter covered. It is sold with the understanding that the publisher is not engaged in rendering psychological, financial, legal or other professional services. If expert assistance or counseling is deemed necessary, the services of a competent professional should be sought.

Royce Publishing
30941 Agoura Rd. Suite 228 Westlake Village, CA 91361
Distributed by Ingram in the United States and international sales
All Rights Reserved.
www.psychonthebike.com

Book Layout ©2013 BookDesignTemplates.com
Cover design by Olivia Carter
Edited by Sam Hidaka

Courage to Thrive/ Trudeau, Stephen. —1st Ed.

ISBN: 978-0-9966136-0-6   Printed in the United States of America

Contents

Victim, Survivor, Thriver 1

Self Esteem Issues 7

Behind Every Bad Behavior is an Unmet Need 11

My Theory 17

Overwhelmed by a Bunch of Grapes 23

Avoid Negative Direction 27

Getting Out of Your Comfort Zone 31

Borrowing Momentum 37

Change is Good 43

Four Reasons to Take Action 49

Withdrawal, Obsession, or Bad Habit? 57

Emotions are Like Crayons 65

Compassion 69

Focus in Order to Thrive 73

Personal Creed 79

Good Habits, Good Goals 87

Homegrown is Best 93

Managing Anger 97

Meditation 103

Overreaction 113

Work Sucks 117

Black Belt Test 123

Taking Down Time 131

Hitting All the Red Lights 137

Development of Relationships 141

Do You Have Something on Your Soul? 149

Your Mind Will Focus on What You Feed it 153

Finding Inner Peace 159

Atonement 165

Random Wisdom 169

The Last Lecture, Leaving Your Legacy 177

A Good Dark Suit 183

Why do I Ride? 189

    Epilogue 193

Gift of Life 195

Conclusion 199

Dedication

To my son, Devin. My wish is that your journey to enlightenment is filled with adventure. You teach me nearly every day about determination. All that I have is yours.

Acknowledgements

I would like to acknowledge the following people for their inspiration, support, encouragement, and motivation in helping me make this endeavor possible. My wife, Mary, for her undying support and belief in me. My son, Devin, for inspiring me to leave a better world for him to live in. Mom and Dad for life.

Will Carter for nearly a lifetime of friendship and adventures. Tammy Bleck for getting me back on track. Jeff Trudeau for always being there and making me finish what I started.

Dr. Dennis Merritt Jones and Jim Cathcart for encouragement and mentoring. David Trudeau, my uncle and teacher. Mr. Fredrick W. Funk III my teacher from long ago, whose lessons I still remember. Rick Allen and Lauren Monroe for friendship that transcends the physical plane.

Dr. Steven Saltzman for his dedication to the teaching craft and stimulating countless minds. Dr. Mark S. Gold for his remarkable work in the field of addictions studies. Dr. Gordon McComb for his genius hands in saving lives.

Praise for Courage to Thrive

"Want to be accepted? Then don't stand out, just stay quiet and fit in. But if you want to be truly deeply happy with your life then Read This Book! Dr.Trudeau shares his own journey from self-doubt and meaninglessness to a life of Thriving, and shows clearly that you can do this too. We all feel inadequate, overwhelmed and uncertain but here are healthy ways to overcome that and they are easy to learn." **Jim Cathcart,** author The Acorn Principle, internationally renowned motivational speaker.

"There are many authors in the world that write and offer advice, and reality is you don't know what to believe anymore. But Dr. Stephen Trudeau is one of the very few authentic writers who have lived the real life, defeat the pain, thrived when the circumstances stood against him, offered his love to people who most needed him, and now he tells the story. Learn from him. This book is a must read for every human soul that has even experienced difficulties in life" - **Dr. Dragos,** scientist, speaker & filmmaker of award winning documentary film THE AMAZING YOU.

"It appears as if Dr. Stephen has been on a roller coaster life journey. Overcoming tremendous obstacles, all the while picking up wisdom along the way. He now shares these precious life lessons with the reader. His concepts about Thriving will inspire a better life." **Dr. Dennis Merritt Jones**, Award Winning author of Your ReDefining Moments - Becoming Who You Were Born to Be, and the Art of Uncertainty - How to Live in the Mystery of Life and Love It.

Introduction

> *"And God help you if you are a phoenix, and you dare to rise from the ash. A thousand eyes will smolder with jealousy, while you're just flying past."* **Ani DiFranco**
>
> *"Before my accident I was a little too...self-absorbed and for me, to now be at the place where I can kinda give back and inspire people. I am blessed. I'm really blessed."* **Rick Allen**

This is the book I needed to read. Many people who know me ask, "How do you keep bouncing back from so many traumas?" There are many answers but after facing trauma, death, and disaster numerous times, I decided to learn from every experience in life and grow from it. The specific strategies and techniques I have learned along the way, I share here.

For me, the most difficult part of growing up was learning to love myself. The self-loathing made it very difficult to engage in positive action and doing things that were good for me. I first needed to understand and eliminate the negative thoughts about my inner self. And that process continues to this day.

You have to learn to love yourself. This will allow you to feel worthy enough to make the investment through the strategies that will be explained in this book. By making this investment, you show appropriate self-love. Then, by living with an abundance of love and joy in your life, i.e. *thriving*, you will also have love and joy left over to share with others.

Why *Courage to Thrive?* Thriving is vigorous existence, and growth throughout our life. We humans wish to thrive, but the circumstances of our life can be challenging. In many of us, these challenges leave us broken or damaged, and we live our lives of quiet desperation, just existing, or barely surviving. I do not wish to just survive, I wish to *thrive*. The important ingredient in thriving humans is courage.

I wanted to document some of the journey I have made thus far in my life. Thank you for joining me and becoming part of my experience. Also included are stories from people that have inspired me. The various tragedies, accidents, abuses, and self-imposed punishments have served to make for a very interesting life so far. And yet I have also been able to craft for myself a life filled with joy and accomplishment.

Many people would be surprised by my darker inner world because, for the most part, I am a positive jovial person. I have chosen, through a lifetime of personal growth, to make each moment a lesson. When I was much younger I embarked on a journey to discover the meaning of life. What I found was that I alone, must find meaning *in* life. I have suffered through pain that most people could not imagine. And yet, here I am, living a full exciting life, filled with love and adventure. I want to share with you what I have learned thus far.

Each time life has handed me a measure of pain, I felt crushed to dust, burned to ashes, and yet I continue to rise again stronger and more energized, reborn like the fabled Phoenix. My belief is not that I am special in any way, but rather that each of us is stronger and more resilient than we give ourselves credit for.

Each of us is capable of growing from our hardships, but it is a choice.

That choice is to display *courage* in the face of disaster or disappointment. Courage is not the absence of fear; courage is what we do in the presence of fear.

Symbolism is important, which is why I have taken the Phoenix as a personal symbol. This symbol represents triumph over adversity. To continuously rise, filled with hope and strength, from the ashes.

When we are met with abuse, tragedy, or accidents, we are clearly in victim status. Through the passage of time and maladaptive coping strategies, we can be considered *survivors*. It is good to survive. However, why would we wish to identify ourselves as merely survivors? The goal is to create, for ourselves, a state of *thriving*. When we are thriving, we are really living. Victim. Survivor. Thriver. That is the path.

Clearly there are events in our lives that are beyond our control. When bad stuff happens, we can correctly identify as a victim, hopefully only for brief time. Being the victim is a cruddy place to be. We need to change that thought as quickly as we can.

Many times, we are incapacitated to some degree, and if we stay a victim long enough, we develop maladaptive behaviors to cope with the pain. Drinking, drugs, escapism in many forms, even the dreaded defense mechanisms of dear Dr. Freud rear their ugly head. Over time and some healing we can shift into survivor mode.

Surviving is obviously good, however, it is limited by our previous injuries and we are kept there by our maladaptive behaviors and defense mechanisms. If, as a survivor, we are challenged or hurt again, we decline rapidly into victim status once again. We become victims and stay vulnerable our whole lives. But, if we can truly thrive, then the next insult to our lives will merely knock us back to survival mode rather than victim status. The journey then is to eliminate the maladaptive behaviors, escape behaviors, and defense mechanisms that keep us as victims or just surviving.

They say that, "whatever doesn't kill us only makes us stronger." This is not necessarily true. Not all people grow from their trauma—some become crippled by it. Too often we witness good, even innocent people, crushed by the weight of tragedy and they did not become stronger. There are times when life circumstances exceed our ability to cope. However, despite the tragedies, the pain, and the suffering, we are charged with deriving some form of meaning from our lives. By doing so, we step out of the victim role and begin to become the architect of our own destiny.

Rick Allen is the drummer for the successful rock band, Def Leppard. In 1985 he was involved in a devastating car accident which resulted in the amputation of his left arm. Rather than end his career, he came back stronger than ever and a changed man. His story if one of triumph in the face of adversity. He got his act together and became a better man and an inspiration to others. Rick is an example of thriving, and growth through trauma.

> *"And more importantly, I wouldn't be the person I am today, I wouldn't be where I am now and I may not even have been here (alive) if it wasn't for the accident"* **Rick Allen**

Later on, Rick found a way to give back in the most meaningful of ways. He and his wife Lauren, founded Raven Drum Foundation, dedicated to helping others through healing drum circle events. They serve those in crisis, especially wounded veterans.

We are not alone. We can and must seek help from our fellow humans. Therapists, friends, teachers, coaches, clergy, and mentors all contribute to our new knowledge. I humbly submit myself as a source, to share what I have learned thus far. Through each of these stories, I will attempt to articulate one or more concepts of how we can regain our personal power. But the most important attribute we will need on this journey is the *courage* to *thrive*!

I am the Psych on the Bike, black belt, psychologist, husband, father, friend, and traveling soul. Thank you for joining me, this is going to be a fun ride!

CHAPTER 1

Victim, Survivor, Thriver

> *"Grateful people may recover faster from trauma."* **Deborah Norville**
>
> *"Someone who has experienced trauma also has gifts to offer all of us—in their depth, their knowledge of our universal vulnerability, and their experience of the power of compassion."* **Sharon Salzberg**

There is a distinct pattern of response to the traumas in human life. The differences between one who is a victim and stays that way, and the person who is victimized yet goes on to thrive, are often a very small yet profound. The differences are made up of attitude, skill, and courage. Our mission on this planet is not just to survive the various difficulties we are faced with, but also to thrive despite the seeming chaos.

Many times, when a person is victimized, he/she goes into a kind of shock. This is a natural response to trauma, and it comes in two forms: the fight or flight response, and the freeze response. Fight or flight is the primitive brain response that allows us to fight off or run away from a tiger or a bear. Adrenalin pumps, the heart races, blood pressure rises, and blood is sent to the extremities in preparation for hand to hand combat or running away as fast as we can. Alternatively, the freeze response is opposite; it's a full surrender to the attack in hopes of survival by playing dead or perhaps splitting the mind from the body.

While these strategies may be a primitive response to overwhelming situations, staying in the victim role can have devastating long-term consequences. Being a victim all the time is a horrible way to live. It places us in a constant position of feeling like we can literally and figuratively be killed at any time, or simply at the mercy of unfair circumstances.

Over time, we can move into the next phase as a survivor. Surviving has been celebrated in many ways because of the horrific abuse and various traumas that some have suffered. My concern for some people lies in the very real possibility that they may identify so completely with survival, that it prevents them from further personal growth.

In order to survive, we often develop "defense mechanisms," as well as maladaptive behaviors. These protect us but also leave us vulnerable to many other insults and injuries along the way. The defense mechanisms are unconscious thought processes that distance us from the pain of unpleasant feelings and awareness. Maladaptive behaviors are often the result of the defense mechanisms' justification of having some pleasure. As an example; people take up drinking alcohol as a way to escape their pain, frustration, and anxiety about life. This strategy can lead to complications and side effects destructive to their lives, family and future.

There has been much study about resiliency. I see resilience as being relatively unaffected by traumatic events or stressful situations. It is neutral. But growth through trauma allows advancement. Finding meaning or creating meaning manifests true strength to thrive. We must develop our strength not just to endure but to thrive.

The problem with using these maladaptive behaviors is that they only allow a temporary surviving position. Just surviving by these means has side effects that lead to further victimization. Smoking to cope with stress leads to health issues, and that leads to more stress. The long-term consequence of merely surviving is being caught in an endless feedback loop between surviving and being victimized.

The last stage is thriving. In order to thrive, we must face our fears. We are called on to abandon defense mechanisms, and maladaptive behaviors. This takes attitude, skill, and courage. Beyond being resilient, we must grow through our trauma to find meaning in our experiences. Not the meaning *of* the experience, but rather find meaning *in* the experience. More on this concept in the chapter on Four Reasons to Take Action.

When one has achieved a level of thriving, any future insult or trauma may knock us down a peg, but into survival mode rather than the victim status. By endeavoring to keep ourselves thriving, we stand a much better chance of weathering the storms without losing everything we have worked so hard to achieve.

So how do we thrive after being a victim? We must process the initial trauma and place the circumstances in perspective. This often requires the help of a professional or a paraprofessional. The U.S. military has found that by implementing a debriefing strategy with soldiers who experience war zone engagements, they were able to reduce the rate of post-traumatic stress disorder, otherwise known as PTSD. For the average person, this means talking to your therapist, or perhaps a member of the clergy to process your feelings of shock, betrayal, and vulnerability. By doing this we are able to discover or create meaning out of the experience. This also changes one's attitude from weak and vulnerable, to one of empowerment and thoughtfulness.

Next, we must also engage in skill building. Through skill building we abandon the need for the maladaptive behaviors and replace them with truly adaptive behaviors, attitudes, and beliefs. Appropriate self-soothing strategies that quiet the mind and give a sense of inner peace are perhaps the most important skills to build. Examples include: prayer, meditation, focus, exercise, thought stopping, and positive affirmations. There are endless specific skills we can apply to our particular situations. Whether you are a business executive, professional athlete, or a stay at home dad. A good therapist/clergy/coach can work out the specifics with you.

Lastly, we must practice *courage* repeatedly in order to make it a new habit. We must engage life without prejudice or fear. Have the courage to fall down again, and again, yet still get up to try one more time. Success is not measured by how many times you get knocked down, but rather by how many times you get back up. Growth through trauma is an emerging field. It is too complex to describe in great detail here, but suffice it to say that those who develop personal meaning out of the traumas of life tend to have greater chances at thriving.

Thriving is an excellent way to live! By living your life thriving, you are achieving your potential in many areas. Thriving means truly living in the moment and drinking in the beauty of life all around us. We are indeed capable of being self-directed and need not rely on fate to lend us a hand. Become the architect of your own destiny. Who you are today is a direct result of the past choices. Who you will be tomorrow is determined by the choices you make today. Choose to *thrive*!

CHAPTER 2

Self Esteem Issues

> *"Self-esteem is made up primarily of two things: feeling lovable, and feeling capable."* **Jack Canfield**
>
> *"Someday, maybe, there will exist a well-informed, well considered and yet fervent public conviction that the most deadly of all possible sins is the mutilation of a child's spirit."* **Erik Erikson**

There are so many of us with damaged self-esteem in this world. By a show of hands, how many of you have self-esteem issues? 1, 2, 10, 50 . . . okay, it looks like everybody here can relate! The curious thing about the commonality of our damaged self-esteem is that no two people have the same story. Our traumas are unique to us; however, something connects us in this seemingly near universal experience. It may not always be trauma; perhaps also it could be the collection of life insults over time that lead to self-doubt. There must be a common moment for us humans.

We experience the world from infancy as inept humans that need to be taught everything. Instinct is for other animals and it serves them well. We must learn by trial and error. And we also learn from our caregivers. Most of us are born nearly perfect and have so much potential. It is the experiences of our lives that create fractures in our core self that eventually develop into self-esteem issues.

The first crack or fracture in our core self is universal, which comes from the moment we first feel the negative energy, disdain, scorn, or disgust from our primary caregiver. Bill Cosby, known as a comedian philosopher before he was known for his bad behavior with women, had a comedy routine built around that moment where God puts the odor in poo poo. For the first time we feel the rejection from primary caregiver where previously everything we did was adorable. This rejection cuts straight to our core. And every insult and trauma, for the rest of our lives, goes straight to that fracture and makes it wider.

For many of us, the collected insults from bullies at school, or bad parenting, various traumas, etc., continue to drive our lack of thriving all throughout our lives. Subconscious or conscious, we develop fear and protective strategies to shield us from further hurts. We don't want to fail, so we rarely risk trying. In psychological terms, we develop defense mechanisms to protect from our self-doubt.

Defense mechanisms are the thoughts (or lack thereof), which serve to distance us from unpleasant memories, thoughts, feelings, and past behaviors and experiences. They reduce immediate anxiety, but being false, often develop into erroneous beliefs such as: "I'm not good enough," or "I can't deal with this stress." Identifying these thoughts and then challenging the erroneous beliefs is critical to breaking out of our self-imposed prison.

Many times in my life I have been confronted with my low self-esteem issues or self-doubt. Who was I (a near high school dropout), to go back to college and obtain a doctorate degree? Who was I to dare to commit fully to love and embrace marriage? Who was I to dare write a book? In each instance I overcame the fear. I humbly submit that because I am a human, I have dignity and have something to offer. If I can do it, so can you!

Working with a mentor or therapist is a good way to begin to open up and understand how and why we have such self-limiting thoughts. The challenge now is, as an adult, to not dwell on the past. Don't get caught in the trap of blaming current life circumstances on our past. While we may haven't had the ideal childhood experience, we now have the power to be the architect of our own destiny.

In further chapters we will discuss various concepts, ideas, and strategies for reclaiming our self-esteem. It's a long journey but worth the effort. Sudden enlightenment will not solve our problems. Only through dedication to a lifetime of personal growth and development will we gain the perspective we are looking for.

Thriving is about going forward. Looking towards growth and throwing away the limitations of the past. Sometimes we get frustrated at techniques that promise change, only to feel let down by the lack of instant enlightenment. I've had clients tell me that they tried meditation a couple of times but didn't get the enlightenment they sought. That is like going to the gym and not getting buff after the first few workouts. It takes time and consistency to see the benefit.

Michelangelo sculpted the statue of David in marble. It is arguably one of the greatest works of art in mankind's history. The detail is extraordinary. When asked how he created David out of marble Michelangelo replied, "I did not create David, all I did was chisel away all the marble that was not David." Like he was frozen in the giant block and just chiseled the ice away!

In the same way, there is a perfect version of ourselves frozen within us. Our job, through the endeavor of self-improvement, is to chisel away all that is not the perfect us. One of my mentors, Jim Cathcart, has a fantastic saying that gives guidance to our actions going forward. *"How would the person I'd like to be, do the thing I am about to do?"* Isn't that brilliant? It's through the act of thriving that we accomplish the goal of finding our perfection and ultimate happiness.

Our self-esteem issues begin in early childhood and are shaped by our traumas, insults, and circumstances. However, our self-esteem going forward is entirely within our control. We also have an opportunity to share this love with others. By giving respect, not teasing or tearing others down, we can contribute to a healthier world.

Thriving is about growing into our potential. Another saying is; "Hell is, at the end of our life, meeting the person we could have become." Our effort to thrive, close that gap so that in the end we perhaps could be looking into a mirror. We become ourselves.

CHAPTER 3

Behind Every Bad Behavior is an Unmet Need

"A boy or girl given the proper guidance and direction – kept busy and constructively occupied during their leisure or free time – will prove my statement that there is no such thing as a bad boy or girl."
Fr. Edward Flanagan

Behind every supposedly *bad* behavior is an unmet need. I modified that concept from the phrase over the entrance to Boys Town, "There are no Bad Boys." Fr. Edward Flanagan, a Catholic priest, who would take in incorrigible boys, founded Boys Town. He created kind of a reform school with a heart that believed young people would find themselves in difficult life circumstances, which resulted in a learned behavior to make poor choices, in order to survive. The success of Boys Town in nurturing youngsters back to productive lives is amazing.

Fr. Flanagan believed deep in his heart that he could draw out the good in any of these delinquent boys. There was a wonderful movie about Boys Town starring Spencer Tracy as Fr. Flanagan and Mickey Rooney as one of the hopeless, delinquent boys. Mickey's character sets out to prove to Fr. Flanagan that he is indeed "bad" right to the core. But in the end, Fr. Flanagan proves to the young man that he only needs to surrender to love to find his inner goodness.

Behind every *bad* behavior is an unmet need, is my belief. And that behaviors do not define us, but rather are an expression of our inner world. But it is true that others may try to define us by our behaviors, thus the axiom: *People may not believe what you say, but they will always believe what you do.* Often in our world, our pain plays a front and center role in our expressive world through addictions, bad habits, and difficult behaviors that affect others. By embracing the belief that there are unmet needs at work, then we can have compassion for others as well as ourselves. The new task is to reveal those unmet needs and give them a voice.

An exercise I use in therapy quite often is to ask what the unmet needs are. What are yours? I know that exercises like this are all too easy to dismiss. It is easier to continue reading, or engage in other distractions. But seriously, what are your unmet needs? Let's write them down.

Unmet Needs

1._____

2._____

3._____

4._____

I know that in my case, I have a need for acknowledgement, a need to be really seen, that my opinion matters. I have a high need to be respected. This comes from a childhood where I felt much less than important and that my opinions were often devalued. Another need is to be loved unconditionally, which would seem to be somewhat universal in the human experience. Some of our needs are universal and others are very specific to the individual.

Another way of identifying unmet needs, is to look at the supposedly *bad* behavior and ask: "What does it do for me?" Like addiction issues, be they major or somewhat less dramatic, we can ask what the drug or behavior does for us. The common needs of escaping, relaxing, avoiding pain, to be less inhibited, have more energy, alter our consciousness, should be relatively easy to identify if we look inward. My previous drug addiction dulled the pain of feeling alone, broken and misunderstood.

What the Behavior Does For Me

1._____

2._____

3._____

4._____

Now that we have identified some of the core needs and issues, what will be do about it? Drugs, alcohol, escape behaviors, anger, shouting, cheating, and all the bad behaviors that cause us pain, come from lack of fulfillment of unmet needs, and we choose simple and immediate means to deal with not getting what we want. We tantrum or escape through the easiest means.

Now comes the heavy lifting, which means that if we are to change or improve our life and relationships, then we must engage in alternate self-soothing strategies and escape behaviors, as well as appropriate coping mechanisms to deal with difficulties. This is where we need to make a list of the alternatives that we know may take longer and are not as immediately satisfying, but they also take courage to make happen.

Earning my black belt in martial arts and getting my doctorate in psychology are examples of long term investments to fill the unmet needs with something positive. In the short term, meditating, gardening, and motorcycle riding seem to do the trick for me. Time to list your long term and short term self-soothing strategies that you wish to employ.

Alternative Self-Soothing Strategies or Behaviors

1._____

2._____

3._____

4._____

This list should be ever changing because we are learning new strategies all the time, but a few core choices seem to predominate. Exercise daily, eat right, meditate daily, live in the now with mindfulness, and exercise infinite patience. Especially poignant would be the skill of communicating in a calm way.

So much of the conflict in our lives centers on communication issues. We say things we do not mean, and then later have to apologize for saying it. The unmet need is to win the argument, make points, or to preserve our idea of self-image. None of these things facilitate good communication and cooperation. Understanding how important our unmet needs are in motivating choices, gives us the power to make those choices deliberate.

This exercise also will allow you to gain understanding of other's behavioral and communication choices. Having empathy for the other person automatically facilitates patience. With patience and kindness we can create safe relationships that foster trust, and problems get solved that way. Thrivers, most often have good communication skills, that begin with understanding that the person they are dealing with is frustrated and not getting their needs met. We do not have to solve their immediate problem, but patience goes a long way towards a solution.

CHAPTER 4

My Theory

"Whatever terrible things may have happened to you, only one thing allows them to damage your core self, and that is the continued belief in them."
Martha Beck

"What's your major?" is the most asked question in college. In graduate school the most asked question: "What's your theoretical orientation?" These questions are asked because they would like to know what type of person you are, and what can be gleaned from your choice. Such as if one were to say, "I am a business major," then we could assume one is planning to invest a lot of time in business. Versus if the answer is, "I am a history major," one could assume that person would be likely to become a teacher, writer, or museum curator.

In graduate school, especially psychology, one's theoretical orientation suggests the type of therapist one would become. With so many exquisitely profound psychological theories proposed by such luminaries as Freud, Jung, Frankle, Rogers, and Bowen, there are just so many to choose from. Following a school of thought can indicate the kind of person you are. Humanist or pragmatist. Insight oriented or solutions oriented.

For me, this question: "What's your theoretical orientation?" was quite frustrating. I knew that giants had walked before me in the field, but I have never been a really good follower. I wanted to make my own mark and perhaps come up with my own equally relevant theories. Just as Carl Jung started out studying with Sigmund Freud, and developed his own ideas, perhaps I too could eventually develop my own valid theory. This of course never manifested but the dream is still alive.

My particular skill seems to be collecting wisdom from various sources, far and wide, across time and culture and synthesizing into digestible bits for my clients. An eclectic approach if you will. Still, perhaps I could come up with a simple mantra or creed that would explain a few things about my work.

Many an hour went into my final answer, and my attempt to not be automatically assessed by an answer that was merely Freudian, Jungian, Adlerian, Ericksonian, Rogerian, or Bowenian. I searched to simplify what I believed a healthy human demonstrated and lived. What I came up with was, one sentence, two commas, equaling three concepts.

My ideas would help me assess if the person standing before me would be a client, or a reasonably healthy person, whether my client still needed therapy, or had learned enough to go it alone. So how would I know when my client had indeed become a reasonably healthy person and no longer needed my services?

Here it is: Know your core self, acquire skills to adapt, to shape your future.

Knowing your core self is the first piece of the puzzle. Discovery of the core self takes time because of the trauma or collection of life insults over time. These insults cause us to develop protective armor in the form of erroneous beliefs and resultant behaviors. We create a long list of adjectives to describe ourselves. The knowing of core self comes from the exercise of eliminating the adjectives that are good, bad, or indifferent. We strip away to the absolute core of the "I am."

Dr. Steve Saltzman, a professor of mine back in undergraduate work, engaged us in a wonderful exercise to achieve this quest for the core self. At the beginning of class he wrote on the board: I AM _____. He then sat down to look over his papers, ignoring us completely. As dutiful and intuitive college students, we all took out paper and began writing furiously. After about ten minutes he got up and asked us what we had come up with.

Each of us took turns presenting various adjectives that he wrote on the board to fill in the space after the I AM_____. "Tall, short, skinny, fat, intelligent, confused," etc., we shouted out to him. "Student, liar, ashamed, sexy, loud, funny," we continued. I thought I was being clever when I shouted out, "Seeker!" From the silly to the sublime, One by one we all got a chance to get something on the board. Each of us were honest, or trying hard to impress. One girl offered, "I am a burrito eater!"

When the board was filled, Dr. Saltzman stood back contemplating for a few moments, then slowly began erasing items one by one. We looked for patterns in what he was erasing and what he was leaving. No pattern emerged and he continued erasing until everything was gone right up to the space after I AM. Then the space was also gone. Leaving simply the "I AM" on the board.

He cleared his throat, turned to us and calmly asked, "Why would you define the totality of your humanity by ever filling in that blank?" "Do not define yourself with adjectives."

Dr. Saltzman further explains from a brief interview I conducted with him; *"As an example, if I were to say that "I am a man," then my core Self is limited by my definition of what the word "man" means. Similarly, if I were to say that "I am angry," then I allow my understanding of the word "angry" to take control of my core Self and it then will act in exactly the way I have told it to act. This is what is meant when we identify our Self with anything—it then tells the Self what to do, feel, think, etc.*

Dr. Saltzman encourages us to work diligently to eliminate our self-definitions in order to truly reach our core self. Another path to knowing the core self is meditation, but we will cover that in its own chapter. For a person who knows themselves at the very core of their being is at peace. This is crucial for true thriving.

Moving on to the next concept of skills that allow us to adapt to the every changing needs of our environment. Adapting to our environment is what we humans have done very well for all of our existence. It is why as a species, we can survive in every climate on Earth. Modern cultural conditions and our own collective arrogance have given us the erroneous belief in creating a non-changing environment for ourselves. By living in this belief, we suffer greatly as the inevitable change happens.

Accepting change is the first step to eliminating the anxiety of suffering. By not accepting the truth (change is constant), we suffer. Accepting the change and adapting to it allows us the freedom to be in concert with the Universe. Thrivers embrace change, in fact they seem to enjoy it. Self-esteem is boosted each time we adapt and overcome life's challenges. We grow in response to the challenge. Those who adapt to the changing of the seasons, the changing of our abilities, the changes in our fortunes, see that the constant is self. By seeing the bigger picture, we are released from the unrealistic belief in permanence and can enjoy the morphing picture right before our eyes.

The last piece of the puzzle is, shaping our future. This is the manifestation of hope. Anne Frank wrote: "Where there is hope there's life. It fills us with fresh courage and makes us strong again." But beyond hope is the firm belief that we can and do affect our lives. That affect is shapeable. The choices I make today will show up in my tomorrow. Be the architect of your own destiny. Believe that your tomorrows are influenced by the choices you make today.

Thriving persons manifest these three things right before us. They have a deep sense of their core self, they adapt with grace and skill to the changing needs of their environment, and they believe and do shape their future. Know thy core self, acquire skills to adapt, to shape your future. This is our task: to engage in the *courage* to *thrive*.

CHAPTER 5

Overwhelmed by a Bunch of Grapes

"No doubt, some people are quantitatively less busy than others and some much more so, but that doesn't change the shared experience: most everyone I know feels frazzled and overwhelmed most of the time." **Kevin DeYoung**

We all feel overwhelmed from time to time. Sometimes we use the phrase, "Ever have one of those days?" So many times I want to change that phrase to, "Ever have one of those lives?" The daily grind can accumulate a tremendous amount of pressure, which can paralyze us. This environmental, social, mental paralysis can become procrastination of epic proportions. So much so that we are completely overwhelmed. Even the littlest things can seem like they take too much effort.

My personal experience as well as what I've learned in my private practice, has taught me that it's the individual perspective that matters here. People try to be helpful by offering solutions, even actual help with said projects and responsibilities. However, it is the person who is afflicted, they have lost hope. They have lost courage. Well-meaning people and their suggestions only serve to reinforce the inner belief that we have failed. The intended encouragement can sometimes seem that much more oppressive.

Homework, housework, bills to be paid, yard work, dog poop to pick up, lose weight, eat better, exercise, letters to be written, phone calls, emails, dinner to cook, clothes to wash, people to see, reports to turn in, and on, and on, and on, and on! The list can seem endless. Most people see the mountain of chores and responsibilities as insurmountable. They fall into despair. And every day the mountain gets bigger. So big the loss of hope turns to helplessness and depression.

I've seen certain animals eat things bigger than one would think possible. Snakes for instance, can unhinge their jaw to swallow prey bigger than their head! Humans, not so much. I've never once witnessed a human unhinge their jaw and swallow an entire bunch of grapes in one bite. However, I've seen humans eat an entire bunch of grapes, one at a time.

I call this strategy, debunching, which I often recommend to my clients. By taking it one grape at a time we can debunch our overwhelming tasks. Life is a process, one thing at a time, one step at a time. Whatever our responsibilities or our goals, we can accomplish great things if we debunch the problems and take them one grape at a time.

We don't need the courage to climb the whole mountain; we only need the courage to take one step. We don't need to eat the whole bunch in one bite; we only need the courage to eat one grape at a time. This strategy requires that the person focus on only one thing at a time.

Avoid thinking about the enormity of the tasks ahead, just start with one thing, anything. For us runners that means just putting on your shoes. Then next thing you know, something has been accomplished. That is the courage to thrive. So take a deep breath, and have a grape.

CHAPTER 6

Avoid Negative Direction

"A lot of people look at the negative side of what they feel they can't do. I always look on the positive side of what I can do." **Chuck Norris**

Don't do that! Don't say that! Don't even think about it! How many times were we redirected as children by getting a negative direction? From the time we are children, the directive emphasis seems to be on what *not* to do, rather than what to do. We are given negative direction, or what not to do, rather than what to do. Don't eat too fast, don't do drugs, and don't fart in public! Our human lives are all about *doing*, we are unaccustomed to *not doing*. It takes special mental gymnastics to effectively comply with negative direction. Don't think of a pink elephant! See? Difficult, isn't it?

If we see a toddler running toward the street or other danger, yelling "Don't run in the street!" will only cheer them on to run faster. They only hear the "Run in the street," or "Run" part of our yelling. Instead we need to give them clear directions "Stop!" "Turn around," and "Come Here." This gives the toddler a new direction and course of action, which is something they are programmed to understand. As adults, our toddler brain is sometimes still in operation. We still struggle to *not do*.

As a small child, my family was moving into a new house (new to us), which we could barely afford. My dad had organized a few friends of his to help us move on a Saturday, and so he and I went to the house on Friday night to make sure it was cleaned up and ready to move in.

I was following around my father while he fixed little items around the house. One of which was a burned out light bulb in the garage. My father wanted to include me in the fixing so he gave me the one and only spare light bulb to hold onto and hand him when he reached the top of the ladder.

"Now remember," he said. "That is the last bulb we have so whatever you do... DON'T DROP IT." I wanted so much to be a good helper and make dad proud of me, but I didn't know how to "Don't drop it." So as awkwardly as a child could, I reached up to hand dad the bulb and fumbled it badly and of course ... SMASH!

My father just stood there in stunned disbelief. Hadn't he clearly told me what not to do? I felt so small and feeble. What I needed was clear, positive direction. And in fact I did get clear positive direction ... "Clean it up, and this time be careful!" Why couldn't he have said that to begin with? Be Careful. I could have done that.

My wife's father used to send her off into the world with the parting shot of "Don't do anything stupid!" It seemed to work for them, but really most kids would be inspired to find a lot of stupid things to engage in. Teenagers take it as a personal challenge to prove that their choices are not stupid, and they wish to also prove that they can be masterful at dangerous things. Drugs, fast driving, unprotected sex are all examples of what we could consider bad choices, but the teen mind believes that bad things only happen to other people.

A better instructional option would be something like what the sergeant on the old TV show Hill Street Blues would say to the officers before they began their day was, "Hey! Let's be careful out there."

Think of all the well-intentioned *don'ts* we have heard as children. "Don't fall down," could have been, "Keep your balance." "Don't talk back," instead of "Be quiet." "Don't hit your sister/brother," instead of "Keep your hand's to yourself." "Don't do drugs," rather than, "Be careful what you put in your body."

Many studies prove that by having open communication with our kids and telling them specifically what we expect from them really works. We need to tell them we expect them to be healthy, to be responsible, to be kind, to avoid the negatives in life. Then we need to catch them doing it right as often as possible. Kids need to be encouraged by the verbal reward and validation of telling them they are doing it right.

When we reach adulthood, there are thousands of *don'ts* to comply with. Don't speed on the freeway, don't cheat on taxes, don't abuse drugs and alcohol, and don't be an asshole!

Better suggestions to focus on are to enjoy the peace of complying with traffic laws, contribute to our social structure, live a healthy life, and be a kind person.

Intellectually, it's not that difficult to reframe negative concepts into positive concepts. Even the title of this chapter was originally, "Don't Use Negative Directions." Challenging myself to take my own medicine allowed the creative solution to use the phrase, *avoid negative directions.*

Many times throughout a person's life there are opportunities to learn life lessons. Teachable moments we call them, and those who take the time to give clear, positive directions can become mentors. As adults we have the opportunity to influence children and set them up for success. But also we should take the challenge to live by example.

The skill of using positive direction is very powerful. Use positive direction anytime anywhere with children of all ages. You might even try it with all the humans in your life and see what happens! Thriving starts with clear directions.

CHAPTER 7

Getting Out of Your Comfort Zone

"If you put yourself in a position where you have to stretch outside your comfort zone, then you are forced to expand your consciousness." **Les Brown**

Each of us has a comfort zone. Our comfort zone is self-defined as levels of stimulation we can tolerate, predictable outcomes to choices, self-soothing strategies that are familiar. The comfort zone, be it physical like where you live and how far you travel, or mental like what TV shows you watch or books and magazines read, or discussion topics, and even emotional situations be they good or bad but predictable, and finally spiritual comfort zone such as structured practice or the absence of engaging meaningfully.

The truth is that if we do the same things over and over again, we will end up with more of the same. We say we want a better life, but most of the time, we refuse to get outside of our comfort zone. If you do what you have always done, you will get what you always have gotten, which is a sentiment attributed to both Mark Twain and Henry Ford.

In many cases, our comfort zone actually shrinks over time. Unless we are expanding, our comfort zone is reducing. If we don't try new foods occasionally, then we begin to eliminate foods down until we have a very limited diet of *safe*, known foods. We lose friends and acquaintances until we become emotionally dependent on a very select few people, and being humans, they eventually disappoint us, precisely because they are living their own lives. We rarely listen to music outside of our genre that we have determined to be *cool* or pleasing to us. Those who despise breathing heavy or sweating, limit their activities and become even fatter and even more unhealthy.

Inside our comfort zone are behaviors, thoughts, and ideas that are known and familiar, or recognizable. Our minds justify these limitations even in the face of some discomfort because it is predictable. This predictability is subconsciously seen as more desirable than the benefits of venturing out into the unknown.

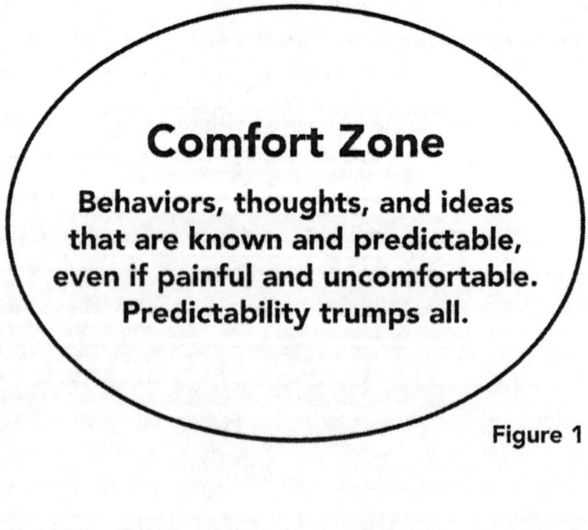

Comfort Zone
Behaviors, thoughts, and ideas that are known and predictable, even if painful and uncomfortable. Predictability trumps all.

Figure 1

Outside of the comfort zone is the terror zone. To venture out of the predictable is terrifying at times. Out there so much can happen and since our fear of the unknown is so powerful, it can be paralyzing and completely overwhelming.

Figure 2

Now for the fun part! Just outside of the comfort zone and just before the terror zone, there exists the *courage* zone. The courage zone is where we display a willingness to tolerate as much or as little discomfort as our current situation and skills will allow. We jump right in or simply put out one little toe.

The courage zone affords us the opportunity for growth and development. This is where confidence is built and self-esteem is developed. By challenging our previously held beliefs and exposing ourselves to the feared stimuli and unpredictability, then thriving begins.

Figure 3

In high school, I had given up trying academically. I never thought I would return to school or be able to get a college degree. Finally at age twenty-six I found the courage to try and take a few classes. Doing well surprised me, and gave me the incentive to keep going, and eventually graduate with honors. As my hunger for knowledge grew so did my confidence. Finally I had the courage to go all the way to earning my doctorate in clinical psychology. All this from a near high school dropout who stuck his toe in the courage zone, and it pulled me in to achievement beyond my hope.

How will you get out of your comfort zone? You could try new foods in order to experience the pleasures that the new tastes and textures bring. Perhaps you could open up emotionally and have challenging conversations with friends and relatives. Take risks that you can tolerate, however small, because each time you get out of your comfort zone, even for a bit, growth is your reward.

Getting out of your comfort zone exposes you to greater opportunities. Thriving is about growth, therefore, we must venture into new territory on all dimensions of our lives to achieve the goal of Thriving. Look to your mentors and heroes and duplicate their risks. We can expose ourselves, by keeping just shy of the terror zone, and living a thriving life in the courage zone!

CHAPTER 8

Borrowing Momentum

> *"In everyone's life, at some time, our inner fire goes out. It is then burst into flame by an encounter with another human being. We should all be thankful for those people who rekindle the inner spirit."* **Albert Schweitzer**

Every human alive has struggled at one time or another with motivation. We may have inspiration and/or obligation, but somehow the motivation eludes us. For many, the lack of motivation has risen to a level of practical paralyzation! The major question for most of us becomes: How will I begin to take action?

We procrastinate in such beautifully inventive ways, to the point of becoming an art form. When I need to be writing, I can find endless ways to be productive without actually writing. The lawn needs mowing, the dog poop needs picking up (not necessarily in that order), find myself playing computer games, or getting caught up on my TV shows. Sometimes I will even start new projects to avoid working on the very thing I need to do!

Many years ago, I was studying with Dr. John Kappas, the founder of Hypnosis Motivation Institute in Tarzana California. I am not sure of his source, but he claimed that only about 5% of all humans are truly self-motivated. The rest of us need outside motivations such as obligation, desperation, or discomfort. And pleasantly enough, we also are motivated by desire, love, friendship, and perhaps the thought of a reward. These things are external. How then, can we hope to change our lives by our own thoughts and actions?

I first came across the concept of *borrowing momentum* while viewing the movie "Awakenings" with Robin Williams. In the movie, a true story of British neurologist, Oliver Sacks, we find him in charge of a group of seemingly catatonic schizophrenics. They are lost to reality and frozen in place. Yet they can move only with the help of orderlies and nurses, but once in their chair, they seem to be unable to really move or engage life. In fact they were suffering from Encephalitis Lethargica, which the good doctor knew would require a completely different kind of treatment, and he had hope for them.

One experiment the doctor was doing was throwing a ball to a patient who could move to catch it but could not throw it. He postulated that the sitting patient could catch the ball by "borrowing" the ball's momentum but had no motivation to throw. Another patient would shuffle along the recreation room but would stop about mid-way and just freeze. They observed that the floor tiles had a checkerboard pattern except where the woman would stop. There was a repair to a large area of tiles that were only white. The doctor and nurses got on their hands and knees to color in the alternating tiles with black markers to continue the visual field. It worked! And the woman was able to continue, "borrowing" the visual momentum of the floor pattern.

Human beings are social creatures, and in our lives, we need to borrow momentum from time to time in order to break the cycle of procrastination or resistance. In the case of exercise or going to the gym, it is well known that if a person has an exercise buddy, they are more likely to show up for the workout out of social obligation. And once we are exercising, we tend to enjoy it and want to go longer.

Sir Isaac Newton's 1st law of motion states: An object either remains at rest or continues to move at a constant velocity, unless acted on by an external force. This relates to us in the sense that a person on a sofa tends to stay on the sofa, and a person who is active tends to stay active. Not a perfect analogy, but close enough.

We must not forget the greatest motivational force known: pride! The pride of accomplishment is internal. We feel good when we accomplish something, especially something difficult. But that feeling is not powerful enough at times to get us started. The reward is too far away to be motivating.

We can indeed motivate ourselves, but often it is only hunger, thirst, or some other discomfort that gets us up off the sofa. Many a good intention exists that never receives action. We promise to "get fit" or to "write the novel" or "mow the lawn" but action never seems to materialize. What we need is a consistent reason to take action, an external force that will give us momentum.

For me to break the procrastination of writing, I had to talk about it with other writers. The amazingly productive author, Tammy Bleck, kindly encouraged me. Her interest allowed me to borrow her momentum and get to writing. Another friend of mine shared with some friends an interest in long distance running, and they were more than happy to be of encouragement and allow him to borrow their momentum. Social interest is very motivating. It ignites the flame within.

Obligation can also play into the picture. I would tell people that I will have a certain number of pages done by a certain time, and they would ask me about it. That social obligation motivated me to type more vigorously. My runner friend would sign up for 5K and 10K charity runs with friends and again, we find the obligation induces more momentum.

Thriving means doing, borrowing momentum from others, asking for help. As social creatures, seeking like minds, companionship, and being responsible to others employs group dynamics. Whether it is getting fit, engaging in a hobby, challenging a fear, or going back to school, we have to acknowledge and perhaps utilize the fact that we need each other. Thrivers tend to surround themselves with inspiring people, people who reignite the fire! Camaraderie is indeed *thriving*!

Thrivers use these strategies to get things done.

1. Structure. They make lists and check them off. They do things consistently each day. Exercise, writing, answering email, various productive behaviors are scheduled. Structure becomes a good habit with its own momentum.
2. Borrowing momentum from others. Keep yourself surrounded by positive, motivated people. Share the experience with others. Borrowing the

momentum of people who are already engaged in action. And being accountable to people socially.
3. Believing in the future rewards. They believe and are motivated by the tangible and the intangible rewards for their efforts. They have vision.

If you employ these strategies, it is bound to pay off. It takes courage to do things that you are resistant to. It takes courage to employ unfamiliar strategies. It takes courage to ask for help. It takes courage to *thrive*!

CHAPTER 9

Change is Good

*"When we are no longer able to change a situation – we are challenged to change ourselves." ***Victor Frankl***

Change schools, change college major, change job, or better yet change career. Many people have displayed the courage to change career midlife. Comic actor Ken Jeong was an M.D. before changing careers to acting in his thirties. Colonel Sanders became successful in the food industry in his mid-sixties. Ronald Reagan was an actor who became a politician in his fifties. Even J.K Rowling was a secretary and on welfare before publishing the first Harry Potter book in her thirties. I changed careers with the help of a fall.

When I graduated high school my job was washing dishes at an Italian restaurant—it's not as glamorous as it sounds. Sure I had an apartment in the worst part of town in the most dangerous neighborhood. And yes, I had criminals for neighbors, but the downside was a lack of career advancement opportunities.

One day I was hanging out with a friend who had graduated high school a year earlier than I. His father overheard me complaining about my job and asked if I wanted to work a real job for real money. Heck yes, so he introduced me at the contractors office of the phone company that Monday morning. Entry level starting pay would be twice what I was getting washing dishes.

Having the prestigious diploma from a last chance continuation high school meant I was qualified, and they handed me a shovel! My job would be to dig holes to put telephone poles into. I'm sure glad I had learned quadratic equations in algebra class. Yes, they had those cool hydraulic truck-mounted augers that could dig most holes, but I would be responsible for the holes where the truck couldn't go. Backyards, the side of a hill or mountain, way off the highway, these locations would be my new office.

I liked to say I actually got into the company below ground level. I even had some business cards printed up that claimed I was a *Senior Soil Technician!* Slowly I worked my way up, literally. I learned how to climb poles, pull cable, and eventually splicing all those multicolored spaghetti looking wires. I earned a good living, too much for a young man with no discipline, and it financed a few years of my hard-core drug addiction.

Eventually I cleaned up, but after a while. I became increasingly dissatisfied with working as a lineman and cable splicer. I had been clean from drugs about four years, but I could not see myself grinding away at this job for the rest of my life.

At the age of twenty-six I enrolled in community college with the intent of taking a couple of classes. I was petrified because I'd been such a dismal high school student. Much to my surprise, I found that with an active interest in my subjects the motivation was completely different. I still had one foot in the construction field and one foot in the academic world, but that was about to change.

Climbing telephone poles is dangerous work, and I had a few close calls. One day in particular I was working a cleanup job, and the foreman wanted us to get out of that neighborhood quickly and move on to the next major job. One mantra we used to live by is this: there is no job so important that we cannot do it safely. I must have read that slogan on a motivational poster at the company office a thousand times. However, that day I let my foreman's insistence on quick work get the better of me.

Not following safety protocols can get you killed. Rushing can get you killed. I took a shortcut, and paid the price. I fell over twenty-two feet, roughly two stories in height. The speed of a fall is remarkable. Before I could say "oh, sh!#" I was on the ground. My injuries included a fractured arm, torn rotator cuff, tendons and ligaments torn, and spinal compression. At the hospital I was in surgery for five hours to repair all the damage. I had been lucky because I most certainly could have been killed.

Lying in the hospital, I received the usual stream of visitors wishing me well and telling me how good I looked. Yeah, looked good for having almost died! After the usual pleasantries, there wasn't much to say. Many of my friends would sit down and begin discussing their relationship with their girlfriend, or troubles at work, or any of the endless trials we humans go through. Apparently, I was a good listener. This gave me the insight and excuse I needed to go at school full time.

The change I was facing was monumental. I couldn't go back to climbing telephone poles, so I figured that I had to forge a new career using my mind instead of my body. I enjoyed psychology and enjoyed helping people. I made the decision to become a psychologist and go all the way to get my doctorate. I think I needed this degree because many people had accused me of never finishing anything I started. This assumption would provoke the rebel in me, driving my determination to take on such an enormous task. This task would turn into ten years of full time schooling.

When I told my friends that I would become a psychologist, most of them laughed. Knowing me from my checkered past, they assumed that no one would seek my advice or take me seriously. Many of these friends were the same ones who had sought my advice when I was laid up in the hospital. But change is so difficult that even thinking of your friends taking on a big change can be scary. I even doubted myself. Maybe they were right, maybe I wouldn't be able to do it. Maybe I didn't deserve it.

My fear of change was because I had such difficulty seeing into my future. I struggled to see myself one, five, or ten years into the future. Most of the time I could only be motivated by the immediate future or the now. While sitting in my cousin Jeff's living room, I told him about my worries. I would be thirty-five years old when I graduated with my doctorate in psychology and only then would I be able to begin my career! He said the most encouraging thing I could have heard at the time. Jeff looked at me saying, "You are going to be thirty-five either way. Are you going to be sitting in my living room then crying that you did not finish school and still had no career? Or are we going to be celebrating your graduation? Your choice."

I found the change to being a serious student was invigorating. Working odd jobs to support myself through school, degrees were being accumulated. I found myself on the Dean's List for academic excellence each semester. Enough self-esteem was being built that I believed I would complete my challenge. I graduated in 2001 with my doctorate in clinical psychology at the age of thirty-six, one year behind my schedule.

I had transformed from an undereducated construction worker into a doctor of psychology. Since then, I have built a successful private practice, hosted radio shows, had my own television show, published articles, written books, toured the country giving seminars on personal growth, and counsel patients at the most prestigious addiction treatment facility in the country.

Change is good. All it took was the *courage* to *thrive*. And a lot of hard work.

CHAPTER 10

Four Reasons to Take Action

> *"If people are good only because they fear punishment, and hope for reward, then we are a sorry lot indeed."* **Albert Einstein**
>
> *"Only one who devotes himself to a cause with his whole strength and soul can be a true master. For this reason mastery demands all of a person."* **Albert Einstein**
>
> *"Thinking is easy, action is difficult, and to put one's thoughts into action is the most difficult thing in the world."* **Johann Wolfgang von Goethe**

My passion in life is studying the human animal, and trying to figure out its motivation.

The fundamental question is: Why do we do the things we do?

Sometimes we engage in behaviors that seem contrary to the seeking of pleasure and avoiding pain. Why would we do something that brings pain or eliminates pleasure? It goes against logic. But does it really? In these instances, it is the power of rejection of the external reward or punishment in exchange for the internal reward of personal mastery. The perspective shifts to that of being in control as more self-rewarding than being dependent on others. Sometimes we also engage in self-destructive behaviors because of loss of hope or learned helplessness.

By studying the human animal I have concluded that there are four reasons to take action or make choices. The first two are related, and known to most of us as *reward* and *punishment*. The reward and punishment model is critical in classical conditioning exercises like the celebrated Pavlov's dogs experiment. Dogs were noticed to salivate to stimuli that were conditionally paired with food. We can control puppy dogs and small children with promises of rewards and threat of punishments.

This can only take us so far; eventually the child grows up and demonstrates rebellion. This is the first indication of being more self-directed. The reward of defiance or being self-directed outstrips the parental rewards and punishments. Being grounded for two weeks is traded for the night out with friends without coming home on time. In this way, the young person learns to reward him or herself, albeit with external sources. And this leads to an adult belief system that one can control the pleasure and pain with external sources.

The external rewards are consumed and the external punishments are either bargained for or lamented as bad luck. When we live our lives seeking pleasure or avoiding pain exclusively, then we are slaves to the external forces that can interfere with the delivery of said reward or punishment. This is the *consumer* model that our culture operates within most of the time. It is also the source of most of our suffering. We want what we can't have, or what we consume comes with consequences and side effects.

This mentality is dependent on the external sources for delivery of the pleasure or pain. The human is forced to behave in certain ways to get the pleasure or avoid the pain, leaving them feeling at times like a victim. Even in rebellion to the parents or authority, a person is dependent on external sources for happiness.

The longer we live this way, the more difficult it is to look inward for the source of true happiness and contentedness. This is why taking personal responsibility and even quiet contemplation like prayer and meditation is so difficult.

The more mature reasons for actions or choices, our reasons three and four, are *altruism* and *personal mastery*. In altruism, like charity, we seek to help or give to others without any expectation of external reward. Personal mastery is the finest reason for action as we are entirely self-rewarded for overcoming obstacles or achieving goals that we set for ourselves. The rewards are internal versus external. When the rewards are internal, then we have a much higher degree of control.

Altruism is giving of self without any expectation of external validation or reward. Charity is the most obvious example. Here a person is giving of self and the reward is internal. There is nothing wrong with the internal reward; in fact it is quite adaptive for our species. We share our blanket with someone who is cold, or our food with a tribe member who is hungry. In this way the internal rewards support the overall health of the tribe and the security of the individuals.

Personal mastery is the most mature and internally driven behavior in our species. When George Mallory, the first person to attempt to reach the peak of Mt. Everest, the highest peak on Earth, was asked why do it, he quipped "because it is there." Why does an average person run a marathon? They do it in order to prove to themselves an ability to conquer something difficult. Any endeavor, from building an international company, or creating a piece of artwork is filled with personal mastery. To learn a musical instrument or to teach children language or even mathematics, fills us with internally generated pride in our accomplishments.

It is not unreasonable to recognize that we humans, need all levels of motivation in order to take action. *Reward, punishment, altruism,* and *personal mastery* combine to fill us with multiple reasons for action that ensure more than our mere survival but facilitate *thriving!*

Reward and punishment most often generate immediate pleasure or pain, and altruism and personal mastery seem to be an investment that takes longer to reap the internal rewards. One of the most important marks of human maturity is the ability to delay gratification of immediate needs for future reward.

A baby cannot delay the gratification of immediate needs. However, as the child grows through the developmental stages of life, combined with lots of practice, delaying gratification is mandatory. If a baby is hungry, it cries. At some point, the primary caregiver begins to make the child wait until after having to take care of other obligations like showering or answering the phone. Then the child is made to wait until lunch or dinner to be fed. Even when the child protests, they eventually learn to wait.

In adolescence, the teen rebels against the perceived unfairness of waiting, and begins to find food for him/herself. If an adult is hungry, they can often wait until the appropriate mealtime to be satisfied. Too bad we have such difficult time with other areas of our life. Perhaps it's time to grow up.

I was working with a young man in middle school, who was struggling with his grades as a result of his depression. While working together, we explored all these areas of motivation so he could be aware of the choices that he was making. He would most often choose the immediate reward of watching TV or playing a video game to avoid his perceived pain or punishment of doing his math homework.

After processing the more mature aspects of motivation his grades started to improve. When asked why he was now doing his math homework, he explained his four reasons to take action. *Reward*, he would get praised from his teacher for turning in the work. *Punishment*, he would be grounded or get detention if he did not complete the work. *Altruism*, better grades would make his mother feel more relaxed. And finally, *personal mastery*, he would actually learn something!

Reward and punishment is a consumer model. The rewards and punishments are external and most often someone else is in control of their distribution. We have to do something the owner wants to get the reward or avoid the punishment, like a parent who wants very specific behavior. This is our modern culture of consumerism. We are told that happiness is out there waiting to be purchased or consumed.

On the other hand, altruism and personal mastery are motivations that show a creative model in the world. They depend entirely on internal motivation. The power shifts to our own mind and soul, desiring to create in the world something. Instead of the adolescent rebellion of providing our own external rewards, the mature adult can create wealth, health, art, music, beauty, family, love, etc.

At some point in the life of each individual, we begin to share with our siblings and friends out of pure love. Then we take on projects with a wondrously creative energy in our playtime world. The pure joy of fantasy play fills us as we manipulate our toys, crayons, and sports equipment. Then in adolescence we pour out our souls in poetry, or identify with our poet musical heroes and rock stars.

Somehow, adolescence is also when many of us become disillusioned with the world and its wonders. We see the pain and injustice in the world. We realize how weird our little world is, how unfair it is. And we come to a dangerous place and time where escape becomes more important that creative endeavors.

It is an interesting paradox that when we feel empty and yucky inside we desperately seek external consumption to satisfy and fill the hole. And yet, the very act of consumption, rewarding for a short time, ultimately makes the hole bigger. The escape through drugs causes short-term pleasure but carries with it long-term consequences. Over consumption of food makes us fat and unhappy. Spending too much leaves us in debt. Being a workaholic isolates our soul from our friends and family. You get the idea, that any behavior which depends on external rewards eventually makes our problems worse not better.

In contrast, the reverse paradox seems to also be true. When we feel lost and alone, digging deep to give to others or pour our energy into creation makes us feel better. When feeling low, the giving to others cheers us up. Or engaging in a creative endeavor to manifest something in the world that did not exist before the effort such as: art, cuisine, construction, music, even a smile will suffice. Personally, I like to work in my garden and nurture the flowers and vegetables which appreciate the attention and grown more vigorously.

Thriving is about being in control. It demands that we take action and avoid the passive victim role. Knowing how we are motivated and how to be deliberate in our choice of action gives a far better opportunity for things to turn out the way we expect. Rather than depend on the winds of fate to be kind to us, we can be the architects of our own success. It takes courage to thrive, courage to engage in the acts that bring personal mastery.

CHAPTER 11

Withdrawal, Obsession, or Bad Habit?

"The average human looks without seeing, listens without hearing, touches without feeling, eats without tasting, moves without physical awareness, inhales without awareness of odor or fragrance, and talks without thinking." – **Leonardo da Vinci**

The process of addiction recovery or simply changing bad habits can be seen in three distinct areas. The Withdrawal, Psychological obsession, and the Kinesthetic values. Kinesthetic value is the body recognition of its parts in relation to each other and its sense of homeostasis. Regardless of whether it is an addiction, abuse, or bad habit, there are phases we go through with different difficulties in each area. Most of us have some behaviors, which started as self-soothing strategies and then turned to something more problematic or even darker.

Physiological withdrawal symptoms range from annoying, to brutally painful, and even life threatening which demands medical care. Psychological obsessions are where the bulk of our work is done. Chasing down the underlying causes of maladaptive self-soothing strategies and replacing them with adaptive strategies leads to better life satisfaction and thriving. And lastly, we need to recognize the kinesthetic habitual behaviors for what they are and how they contribute to returning to past maladaptive behaviors.

The medical/physical withdrawal symptoms will go away with the passage of time. This is where the initial detox period of an addiction is most critical. Enough time away from an addictive substance and the toxins leave the body and we eventually return to a certain homeostasis. Anyone who as ever quit smoking cigarettes will tell you how grumpy they got for the first two weeks after quitting, but eventually found new peace in the healthy lifestyle.

There are many physiological responses to other substances that are not identified as illicit. It can be very surprising to find out how difficult it is to change or even quit using sugar, or eliminating caffeine. This is because our bodies are amazing at adapting to differing foodstuffs, and chemicals. We can adapt in many different circumstances and changing that adaptation can be uncomfortable but will happen given enough time.

The psychological obsessions, how they develop, and treatment options are the domain of the field of psychology. We ultimately have to understand the *why* of how we are not getting our needs met, and seem to need the maladaptive behaviors to just survive. This thinking is because we have not yet learned how to truly thrive.

Abraham Maslow postulated that the human is seeking to self-actualize. That is, we are on a path of expanding our consciousness to become wise and at peace. I feel that the reasons we have not embraced optimal life behaviors is because we are focused on the immediate needs of safety and other priorities. According to Maslow, our education is not complete, our minds are having not yet fully self-actualized. However, by engaging in therapy and acquiring new wisdom, we will self-actualize. It is a choice.

Now we will focus on the bad habits that are deeply ingrained through kinesthetic value. Dr. Mark S. Gold focused his research on the dopamine connection of addiction. This field of study opening up allowed for additional substances and behaviors to be included in the definition of addiction, whereas in the past, only chemicals that caused withdrawal symptoms were considered addictive. In fact, we now have a greater understanding of how dopamine is implicated in the subtle rewards for many behaviors that are now labeled as *process addictions*.

A quick note here on process addictions. These are classified as problematic behaviors such as; sex addiction, gambling addiction, food addiction, spending addiction, etc. These are also referred to as *soft addictions*, behaviors that are problematic in a person's life. How do we know there is a problem? When there is clinically significant impairment and/or distress in some area of life, usually work, relationships, or leisure activities. A question that might help indicate a problem would be; "Has my life become unmanageable or painful in any area?"

When smokers try to eliminate cigarettes they are not fighting the nicotine but also battling the ritual. The nicotine is the chemical in cigarettes, which causes the physiological addiction. The withdrawal from nicotine is very uncomfortable but it will pass within a couple of weeks. The psychological obsession with cigarettes often has to do with looking cool, control issues, or boredom.

The bad habit or kinesthetic issues are many such as: what to do with one's hands, and all the rituals that go into supporting the habit. This is why replacement behaviors seem to help like, eating sunflower seeds, or holding a pencil between the fingers.

We need to be aware of what is triggering our cravings and behaviors. One of the most important discoveries has been the dopamine connection. Dopamine is a neurotransmitter that is implicated in the reward system of the brain. Dopamine is responsible for rewarding certain behaviors that are supportive of survival, so it is a very primitive mechanism and vital to life.

In prehistoric times, when a person found some honey, which contains very tasty concentrated calories, the brain would be rewarded with dopamine to increase the likelihood of repeating this survival behavior. Primary reinforcers are critical to not only the individual but also the survival of the species. These primary reinforcers are things such as food, drink, and pleasure.

Dopamine is released to reward the survival or primary behavior, but what we have recently learned is that dopamine is also released for behaviors that lead to the primary reinforcer.

For instance, picking a restaurant, opening the menu, choosing and item, ordering, and finally eating. The rewards for successfully closer approximations of the goal develop a conditioned behavior through chaining these events.

A rat poised to learn a maze does not understand that there is a big food reward at the goal line. So the researcher first entices the rat with a seed or small food pellet a short way down the maze at a landmark. Then another small reward further down at another landmark and so on to encourage the rat to explore the maze. Eventually the rat figures out that there are a series of small rewards available for the exploration. Through trial and error it finds the big reward.

The researcher next slowly eliminates the small rewards in order to get them to run the maze for the one big reward. Even though the seeds or small food pellets have been removed, the rat is rewarded with small dopamine rewards by its own brain after passing each landmark.

Not only are we being rewarded for our food consumption, drinking, various pleasures including sex, music, spending, drugs, etc. But we are also being rewarded with dopamine in small and large doses for the primary rewards as well as all the seemingly insignificant pieces of the rituals that, chained together, support the behavior. No wonder it's so difficult to break ingrained patterns. Imagine the many thousands of repetitions of these behaviors that we have engaged in!

The following is a tale illustrating the power of the kinesthetic or body movement value.

Once upon a time, in a land we all know, an older man was visiting his doctor. His wife was present as the doctor discussed his high blood pressure. The doctor gave him his prescription for the medication that would lower his blood pressure, with an admonishment that he should cut down on his intake of salt. The man's wife nudged him in the side saying: "See? I told you all that salt wasn't good for you!"

Back at home, the man continued to shake salt on all his food, without even tasting it first. His wife would nag him to cut the salt down but the man refused to slow down as he thought food tasted too bland without it, and life was too short for bland food. Back at the doctor a month later, his blood pressure was nearing the critical threshold. Still he would not stop shaking salt on his food.

Soon the man's wife developed an idea. She unscrewed the cap to the saltshaker at home and placed a piece of clear plastic tape covering the holes from the inside. Placing the saltshaker back on the table she waited to see if her husband would notice. That evening during dinner, she remembered to nag him a bit about the salt as he shook it all over his food.

After a month or so, the doctor was able to report that the man's blood pressure was dropping and getting into the healthy zone. The man felt vindicated that it wasn't the salt after all. Although one day he asked his wife mid shake: "Honey, why does the level in this saltshaker never go down?" They both had a laugh as he figured out her ruse. But the point was made, that it wasn't the salt he was addicted to, but rather the shaking. He had a greater need for control and the kinesthetic value of shaking.

When we are changing habitual behaviors in ourselves, it would be wise to be aware of the previously dopamine-rewarded behaviors that chained together made up the ritual of our past behavior. This is why we can be triggered by seemingly innocent behaviors. And by being aware, we can also use our cognition to change the association deliberately. We can be empowered to use new rituals in order to get a different reward of self-control and personal mastery. Taking a moment to really absorb the beauty, the smells, the textures of what we are doing in the now, can help us regain conscious control of the dopamine reward system to shape the behaviors we desire.

A good example of this would be how we prepare for going to the gym or engaging in a sport. The special clothes we wear like the new shoes or running shorts can be a focus, also lacing up the shoes and paying attention to the smell of new items. We can notice the beauty of our neighborhood as we run or bike along the streets and trails, and finally enjoying the thrill of crossing the finish line of a local charity event race.

Another strategy would be to focus on one of the strongest primary reinforcers, food. Take the time to enjoy the shopping in the produce section, smelling the aroma of the produce. Stopping to really taste our food and savor the flavors and complexity.

This mindfulness of our internal reward system is an act of thriving. Thriving is concerned with growth, development, and personal mastery. The rewards are internal and under our control. Imagine having conscious control of your internal reward system! And to create new adaptive, and healthy habits that support your efforts to thrive.

CHAPTER 12

Emotions are Like Crayons

"One forgets words as one forgets names. One's vocabulary needs constant fertilizing or it will die." **Evelyn Waugh**

Have you ever noticed how when a child is expressing their emotions, they tend to use a very limited range but also feel and express them with great intensity? My observation over many years of doing individual and family therapy is that children and adults really benefit from expanding their emotional vocabulary. With children, it is up to the adults in their lives to help them with the task of coming up with alternatives to the same overused emotions of sadness, joy, anger, and love. Humans need to find ways to open up and explore an expanded emotional vocabulary.

Another way of explaining this is with crayons. When a child goes to a restaurant, the wait staff will often bring over a placemat child's menu with activities on it with two or three crayons with which to draw. The challenge to create any kind of realistic expression is very limited. What kind of picture can you really draw with only three crayons? Not a very interesting one.

Now imagine how much better a picture can be drawn with the box of eight crayons. Or the bigger box of twenty-four? Perhaps we splurge and get the really cool box of sixty-four crayons, with that many choices, a great and colorfully varied picture can be created. And for the really ambitious, get the deluxe box of 128 colors with the cool built in sharpener!

Emotions are like crayons. The fewer we have available, the less we are able to express. As the number of choices of colors increases, the more accurate, varied, and interesting our art and emotional expression becomes. At the restaurant we are lucky if we get the blue crayon. With the box of twenty-four, we have blue, indigo, and light blue. But in the deluxe box of 128 there is blue, sky, navy, teal, azure, baby, and many more.

With an expanded emotional vocabulary we have a greater degree of specificity with which to express our inner world. This is more likely to lead to us feeling understood by others and not so alone in our thoughts. Each word has subtle differences that share a more nuanced experience. Humans wish to be understood and for people to *get* them.

If we only have the word *angry* to describe feeling unpleasant, then angry we will be. What is put out is often taken back in. To say, "I'm angry" requires the anger to be backed up with behavior. That behavior is different for each word that the person is fully committed to. In 1966, Abraham Maslow described this concept known as: The Law of the Instrument thusly: "I suppose it is tempting, if the only tool you have is a hammer, to treat everything as if it were a nail."

Imagine if you had a vast array of emotions to choose from to more accurately describe your inner experience. Then you could be angry, or upset, disappointed, frustrated, annoyed, exasperated, surly, irritated, pained, jealous, confused, discouraged, and so on.

Each word has specific meanings, feelings, and behaviors associated with it. Developing the skills to identify how you really feel, and being able to express it appropriately to others, is of paramount importance to truly being understood.

Children and adults benefit from the opportunity to develop an expansive emotional vocabulary, with the result being greater understanding and control. How do we do this? By talking out loud about our own emotional process.

When we begin to feel the emotions bubbling up, then say out loud what we are feeling and modify it if it doesn't sound quite right. "I am beginning to feel angry, no that's not it. I must be feeling more frustrated. Yeah, that's it frustrated." Follow that up with appropriate choices for self-soothing and problem solving and we become a living example others, especially the children.

The greatest opportunity to expand our emotional vocabulary is with the tremendously rich and valuable conversations in therapy. Psychologists, marriage and family therapists, social workers, etc., all have specific training in providing alternative interpretations of our inner experiences. They help us with expanding our own emotional vocabulary to more precisely express what we are feeling.

The skill and act of reading is the single most important tool that allows expansion of vocabulary. Reading exposes us to more than mere conversation. Read quality literature on personal growth and development. There are hundreds of thousands of words in the English language, most of them technical language and yet, the average high school graduate has a working vocabulary of about 15 thousand words.

The average college graduate has a working vocabulary of about 30-40 thousand words! If we read challenging material, rather than just pithy blurbs about celebrity gossip, then we experience a larger intellectual world.

In order to open our inner world, we need more words. Metaphorically, we need more crayons in our box so that we can create more beautiful, varied, and essentially more accurate pictures of our inner world. Thriving, means to grow. And by growing we gain more control of how our world looks.

CHAPTER 13

Compassion

"Love and compassion are necessities, not luxuries. Without them humanity cannot survive." **Dalai Lama**

Dr. Gabor Mate, eminent addiction specialist, describes all addiction as escape from pain. To heal, we must be with the pain. And only in the presence of compassion can we feel the pain safely. I believe that addictions, obsessions, self-sabotage of all kinds are the escape from pain. Dr. Mate asserts that the act of escaping from pain only causes more pain.

We need to cultivate compassion in our lives, for ourselves and for others. Drawing people into your life that will allow you to feel the pain in their presence is essential for feeling safe. In the absence of this compassion, we feel terribly lonely and misunderstood. One could then be justified in making this lonely pain go away with the various self-sabotage pain escaping behaviors.

When my son was born 12 weeks premature, our family was thrown into chaos. I thought that my perfect world was coming down around me. At that time, I was clean from drugs for about twelve years. I was in graduate school, had bought my first house, married the love of my life, working a good job, and we were going to have a baby. It would seem as if the bargain of quitting drugs and then my life would improve was coming true.

Devin, my son, was in the neonatal intensive care unit (NICU) at Children's hospital in Los Angeles, preparing for the first of several surgeries that would save his life. And if there was ever a time where I could have relapsed to escape the pain, and that would have been it. Thankfully, I had invested many years in appropriate self-soothing strategies such as meditation. However, this day was particularly painful and I had no safe place to experience the pain.

As I sat on a hard plastic chair in the NICU, my head in my hands, I saw two white athletic shoes approach me. I assumed it was a nurse, and she gently put her hand on my shoulder. As soon as she touched me, the flood of tears began. The pent up pressure released and I wept deeply for what seemed like an hour but in reality was only about three or four minutes.

I never looked up to see who it was, but she would hand me tissues without a word the whole time I cried. When I collected myself and my fistful of tissues, she patted me twice on the shoulder and left.

Never knowing who that kind nurse was who showed me so much compassion was a blessing. I treated all the nurses, throughout our over two months with them, as if they were the one who gave me such an incredible gift. The relief I felt was tremendous. Nurses truly are *angels of mercy*.

During that same period of time in the hospital, I experienced another moment of compassion from my son's neurosurgeon, Dr. Gordon McComb. He gave me the opportunity to be with my pain, which then transformed into strength and hope.

Dr. McComb was hesitant to predict too rosy a picture for Devin's future, but he was quite confident in dispelling the previous doctor's prognosis from our local hospital. They had indicated that Devin, if he even survived, would be so profoundly disabled that he would have no quality of life. Dr. McComb scoffed at this assertion and told me that he could almost guarantee that Devin would run, laugh, and play in our backyard someday. This is what I needed, a bit of hope given by a person with compassion.

We each have different hardships to deal with throughout our life. If you could see the five, ten, or twenty traumas laid out on a timeline of your life, then you would see the inevitability of the challenges. But you would also see the great many joys that are available as well. By cultivating compassion in ourselves, and seeking to be in the presence of compassionate people, we can prepare to feel our pain and not store it. By storing it, we allow the pain to consume us from the inside.

We cannot always count on the random compassionate person to be there in the hour of our need. One of the best ways to feel that compassion is to seek out qualified therapists, mentors, or clergy that have the training to be able to contain our emotion at those times. Psychologists, marriage/family therapists, and social workers are trained in compassion. Their job is to provide a safe container for emotion to be felt.

When we begin the healing process, at some point, it makes sense for us to share the compassion. Giving back to others is tremendously empowering and moves us closer to thriving.

Part of why I became a psychologist is because of an immense desire to help others who are suffering. To lessen their grief, pain, troubles, and loss of hope. I wish for people to heal faster and not suffer in the same ways I did. I wish to share what I have learned about healing and ultimately, thriving. By showing compassion, our hearts grow and the world is a better place.

CHAPTER 14

Focus in Order to Thrive

"Concentrate all your thoughts upon the work at hand. The Sun's rays do not burn until brought into focus." **Alexander Graham Bell**

How many of us really ever focus? Focus on the task at hand? Perhaps focus our energies to accomplish a profound goal? So much of life is just getting through. Survive the day's tasks and challenges. We spend enormous amounts of energy attempting to make ourselves comfortable. We struggle to decide what to eat, what to wear, where to go. We do battle on the freeway to find the perfect lane, we switch channels on the radio every two minutes in a vain attempt to find the best song or talk show that reflects our ridiculously specific values.

Why must we get home at the end of the day feeling like we have just barely survived another day? We live at the edge of disaster and survival. When do we get to shine?

I have twice had the supreme pleasure of seeing master Ukulele player, Jake Shimabukuro, in concert. He draws packed crowds, standing room only. Just Jake, and his beautiful Ukulele. I cannot help but be amazed that with just four strings, he captivates large audiences.

An audience waits to be amazed and he holds them spellbound with his unique interpretations of originals and cover songs. We are witness to a human thriving right before our eyes. His gift to us is the sonic journey, with the music moving us emotionally. I notice that the music moves him as well. If you have not yet heard of him or his music, check him out on Youtube right now. I will wait for you to return.

(Whistling softly to self) Oh you are back? Good.

Can you believe how good this guy is? He demonstrates perfect focus. During each concert, Jake banters, telling stories between each song, but as he begins to play, the magic is invoked. Slowly he takes a deep breath, eyes closed, and enter the zone just as his fingers began their magic dance. Like a samurai drawing his sword with deliberate swiftness, like a potter concentrating on the emerging vase at his wheel, like a basketball player shooting his perfect three pointer, he applies his entire focus to the task at hand.

I make the case, that in order to move beyond just surviving, we must have the courage to thrive. The courage to engage in the effort it takes to become brilliant at something, to find a purpose to our existence, beyond mere survival. We may never rise to the amazing levels of admired musicians, athletes, martial artists, poets, or inventors. However, we must engage our lives with the attempt to be amazing. Perfection is unattainable, but in the pursuit we find meaning.

Marianne Williamson in her poem, "A Return to Love," challenges us with these words. "... *who am I to be brilliant, gorgeous, talented, fabulous? Actually, who are you not to be? You are a child of God. Your playing small does not serve the world. There is nothing enlightened about shrinking so that other people won't feel insecure around you. We are all meant to shine ...*"

We all have talents. Talents, which get rusty from misuse. Our excuse is that we don't have the time to practice. We don't have the time or energy because of the Herculean tasks of survival. We say to ourselves: "If only I could remove these barriers to my success, I could be great but, I am a victim of circumstance, so I can't." And yet, we all recognize that we do have talent. We could be good at something. Why not take the chance? Because in taking that chance, to apply oneself to improvement, weather it is music, cooking, athletics, academic thought, poetry, art, science, or gardening, we can find our deeper selves. We can thrive.

I challenge you to take the risk. Yes, I am aware that not every one of us has a hidden *supreme* talent, but isn't it worth the effort to maximize those talents we do have? I read somewhere that if you spent 15 minutes a day on any focused task, eventually you would become an expert at that task. 15 minutes a day, on something you enjoy often turns into a much longer period of time.

Musicians show us the end result of many thousands of hours of practice. The same goes for athletes, chefs, scientists, etc. The sad truth is that most of us spend hours each day unfocused on mindless television, pointless video games, and pursuing our love of fast food. I challenge you again, to take the risk and show the courage to thrive.

A lot has been made of being in the moment. Perhaps overused to the point of losing its powerful message. Or perhaps we shun the spotlight of greatness and would rather that our goal is to participate in the mundane, perfectly. Many hours spent in the garden most often turns into a flower filled wonderland. The accumulation of our focused effort can have spectacular results.

By being in the moment, applying focused effort, we have goals, and the closer to those goals we get. A marathon is run one step at a time. A castle can be built one brick at a time. A symphony can be composed one note at a time. When we do these things we create our moments to shine.

Before I had a child, I fantasized about teaching them martial arts. I wanted them to feel the confidence of being able to defend themselves. I knew they would also gain the added benefits of focus and personal mastery of tasks. The martial arts demand focus. My son, Devin, has cerebral palsy and I therefore thought he would not be able to participate. However, he was interested and I have trained with him through the years.

An example of focus demonstrated in the martial arts world is board breaking. It requires focus more than strength to avoid injury. Devin and I set out to master this skill with many short episodes of practice. Many people said I was crazy for trying to teach a disabled kid to break boards. However, I knew success would translate into other areas of his life and also bring self-confidence. It took a while but he has done it!

Jake Shimabukuro takes us on a sonic journey through his dedication and focus. He spent countless 15 minute sessions, or dare I say hours, to accomplish his goal of filling the world with beautiful music for our enjoyment. He is an example of what any of us can do if we put our minds to it. With just four strings he can captivate an audience and fill the room with his focus. My own son, with a profound disability has accomplished something special. What will you do today to improve your life? What will you do with 15 minutes each day? How will you develop goals to *thrive* in your life, not just survive?

CHAPTER 15

Personal Creed

"I won't be wronged. I won't be insulted. I won't be laid a-hand on. I don't do these things to other people, and I require the same from them." **John Wayne**

Everyone lives by principles. They can be positive or negative but they guide behavioral choices and justify actions. My observation of people who thrive is that they are specific with their principles and often write them out as a personal creed.

I have used this idea as an exercise in my group therapy sessions with really excellent results. The exercise is to look for inspiration, then to define the principles and ideas that you wish to live by. Evaluating and reevaluating over time to make sure the principles continue to be valid. This should be a living document for yourself. Something that can change over time as your wisdom grows and life experiences teach new lessons.

My drug addiction came to an end in a very private and profound way. Years of escape from hopelessness and severely damaged self-esteem had left me completely drained and empty.

My strategy of living hard and having fun until I would die had culminated in a very sad, grotesque cocaine binge of over three months. My brother Joey, had committed suicide in January, and by April, I was spent. Numbing myself beyond ridiculous proportions to kill the pain. My hope was that I would overdose and have a heart attack that would end my suffering permanently.

The years of abuse had taken its toll on my mind and body. I awakened that morning to find that something was different. Sitting on the edge of my bed, I was looking at my hands and I just knew that was my last day on the planet. I did not know how, but I just knew that I would die that day.

Looking again at my hands, I felt the molecular bonds that held me together were loosening. As if my abuse has dissolved the connections between every atom in my body. I was disintegrating. I was dying.

As I sat there contemplating my demise, a thing I had wished for quite a while, my mind began to split. Call it *amphetamine induced psychosis* if you will but it was very real to me, as separate but equally strong elements of my personality began to argue.

On the one hand was the self-destructive side with utterly destroyed self-esteem, bereft of any hope and embracing death. On the other hand was that small glimmer of self-preservation and desire for a quality of life. Mediating between was a wisdom that would challenge me to change.

One voice ordered, "Admit you want to die." I refused, "Admit you want to die or you will indeed die. The only way to avoid dying today is to fully feel your hopelessness." After an internal struggle, I did admit to myself my suicidal ideation and admit that virtually all my behaviors for the past ten years were leading me to death. "But I want to change my mind! Can I do that?" "Yes," the voice said, "but there is no deception allowed here. If you really want to change your mind, then what are you now going to do? How will you change your life?"

I thought for a very long time, tears streaming down my face because I knew that if I did not get this correct, I would die. It would be too simple and disingenuous to simply promise to quit drugs. It had to be more profound. Slowly and idea formed. And it came to me.

The idea was deeper than words and I was only able to craft the forthcoming words much later, but deep inside I knew that in order to live, I had to stop killing myself. My new first principle, the beginning of my personal creed would be: *I will only engage in life affirming behaviors, I will avoid life disconfirming behaviors.*

The psychosis lifted, and I felt the weight of the world lift off my shoulders. Something had changed. I had changed. I changed my mind. My previous hopelessness and despair gave way to a determination to only engage in life affirming behaviors.

This principle of engaging in life affirming behaviors has guided my choices ever since. I never returned to drugs because they were so obviously not life affirming. Throughout the rest of my life, I have gathered several more items for my personal creed. I will next share them with you, but only as an example. My hope is that you will take on the task of changing your life and commit to living a personal creed that guides your behavioral choices which will foster thriving.

My personal creed, principles to live by:

1. I will engage in life affirming behaviors, I will avoid life disconfirming behaviors.
2. I will leave the world/people better than before I arrived.
3. Character is what I do when no one is watching.
4. I am responsible for my own happiness, and others are responsible for their own.
5. I will engage in a daily spiritual tradition.

The first one we have already discussed and it is the foundation of how I choose to live my life. I find great comfort in that principle because if I am ever confused or stumped, then I can evaluate my choices and usually come to the correct choice.

Number two evolved out of my observation that we humans are often *takers*. I had spent too much of my life taking, consuming, and expecting sustenance from the external world. I vowed to leave the world a better place and to leave people enriched when I interacted with them. This gave me a moral footing. While I had been an addict, I had made the world more chaotic and messy. I had contributed to the decline of many people in my life. Even though I thought that my behavior only hurt myself, in fact I had hurt a great many people. This principle allows me to make up for past sins. It can be as simple as this quote, "If you see someone without a smile, give them one of yours." Attributed to Zig Ziglar and Dolly Parton.

Number three, the principle of character being defined by actions whether or not I am observed. My behaviors should be consistent. I try my best to not engage in behaviors that I would be embarrassed by if I were observed. Character is defined more by what a person does in the absence of social pressure. The choice is up to the individual based on principles held dear and deep.

Taking responsibility for my own happiness is the fourth principle, and it was particularly difficult to come by. For many years of my life, I had the mistaken belief system that people or things external to me could make me happy, and that I could make someone else happy, and concurrently I expected the loyalty and logic of others to make me happy. Failure after failure left me very confused.

When it was clear to me that I am responsible for my own happiness, then I could let go of the expectation of someone or something making me happy. I was free! I had become free of the responsibility to *make* others happy, they are responsible for their own happiness as well.

And lastly, I must engage in daily spiritual tradition. This was borrowed from Marianne Williamson. She is powerful spiritual teacher and author. I had the privilege of attending a seminar she was giving. At the end of her presentation, was a question and answer period wherein Ms. Williamson answered each question but also asked each person what their daily spiritual tradition was. The implication was that many of our problems could be resolved with this practice. Any spiritual practice will do. Prayer, mediation, deep breathing, self-hypnosis, or simply sitting still for a few moments in full gratitude for the blessings in life.

My personal creed is indeed a living document. It has grown over the years, however slowly, to just 5 principles so far. I expect to add more as time goes on. My choice is to add only those principles that stand the test of time, strike me very deeply, or develop out of other more simple principles. Your choices can be any that you wish. The point is to be deliberate and write them down. They are more powerful that way, they become more solid and focused.

Many great leaders and successful people have written a code to live by. George Washington tried to live his life as the perfect 18th century gentleman. There are many books about his seven principles of liberty as well as his 110 Rules of Civility & Decent Behavior in Company and Conversation.

Benjamin Franklin has his 13 virtues or principles for success. He tried to follow them but many times failed, however, he would return to these principles to get back on track and try to become a better person. Although listing his principles here would take up too much space, looking up his creed is well worth the easy research.

Even Mother Theresa, the champion of the poor and starving, had a creed written on her wall. And again, easy to look up on the internet as another example to inspire your work. A set of principles can be contained in a poem, a song, the Ten Commandments, etc.

Most people, who thrive, take the time to write out their creed, or principles to live by. The exercise of writing them drives them deeper into your core self. This causes them to be more alive, more solid, and more likely to be followed. Thriving is about living the best life available to us. And we must take advantage of the tools that make that best life possible.

CHAPTER 16

Good Habits, Good Goals

"Motivation is what gets you started, habit is what keeps you going." **Jim Ryun**

"What you get by achieving your goals is not as important as what you become by achieving your goals." **Zig Ziglar**

Life is like riding a unicycle on at tightrope wire. And just when you think things are going smoothly, the universe grabs a hold and shakes that cable vigorously, seemingly to knock you off! Hopefully we regain our balance and recover but then the universe challenges us again and again all through our journey of life. It would seem that we should be doing what we can to prepare for these challenges, by investing in ourselves and our adaptive skills. This is how I begin my presentation on developing good habits and goal setting.

Back to the image of sitting on a unicycle, balanced on the tightrope. The first concept to help us here is that there is usually a force, which propels us forward even if we stop pedaling for a brief time. This force is called momentum. Our lives are governed by habits both good and bad. I am sure we are aware of how bad habits slow us down. The momentum is generated by the effort expended on *good habits*. Good habits keep us moving in the right direction.

The second concept is goal setting. Goals have the value of pulling us into the future. Our goal is in the future and we have to travel a specific path to get there and engage in specific actions to manifest the goal. I like to imagine goals are like a bungee cord anchored at our waist and the other end attached to the goal. We can feel the pull of the elastic towards our goals.

So we have the momentum of good habits pushing us forward, and goals pulling us into the future. This is how we overcome the challenges the universe has in store for us. When we do not have good habits then it is easy to lose focus and direction. If we do not have appropriate goals, then we have restless wandering. These conditions are certain to lead us into unhappy choices.

I have found that it is of immense value to take stock in what we currently have going on in our lives. We need to evaluate by honestly looking at our current state of good habits and goals. Let us do that now through a lens that might put things in perspective, which will set us up for the more advanced exercise coming later.

Start by listing your good habits and organize them by physical, mental, emotional, and spiritual behaviors. Yes, I am absolutely sure you are already engaging in some good habits.

Physical:_____

Mental:_____

Emotional:_____

Spiritual:_____

An example of good habits; Physical = brushing teeth daily, exercising, and avoiding too many sweets, Mental = read good books, further education, and avoiding too much profanity, Emotional = saying kind things to people, random smiles, and laughing often, and Spiritual = saying daily prayers, daily mediation, and giving thanks.

We have many good habits as well as bad habits that develop over time in our lives. I am sure most of you brush your teeth every day right? That is a good habit. A bad habit is smoking cigarettes. Good habits give momentum toward your goals and bad habits are detrimental to our momentum, in fact having the opposite effect of dragging us backwards.

Now let us work a bit on your goals. They too should be divided up by physical, mental, emotional, and spiritual dimensions. But in this exercise I think it would also be valuable to divide them further by short, medium and long-term goals. That way, the enormity of certain goals is broken down into more attainable pieces.

| Goals | Short | Medium | Long Term |

Physical:_____
Mental:_____
Emotional:_____
Spiritual:_____

An example of a physical goal broken down would be: Get in shape = long term. Run a 5K = medium term. Go for a run = short term.

An example of mental goal broken down would be: Finish college degree = long term. Going consistently to classes = medium term. Registering for school = short term.

An example of emotional goal broken down would be: Improve quality of relationship = long term. Weekly quality time = medium term. Making the phone call or set a date = short term.

An example of spiritual goal broken down would be: Be more at peace = long term. Meditate or pray daily for 20 minutes = medium term. Pray or meditate today for 20 minutes = short term.

A brief Google search will turn up many examples of goals in each of these areas. I encourage you to find goals that are meaningful to you and your experience of life. Make it personal. This is a journey of personal growth and development. It is a lifetime commitment. Thriving means to grow vigorously which requires a certain amount of effort be invested.

One of the beautiful aspects of this process of identifying good habits and then structured goal setting is that the achievement of these goals turns them into good habits! The goals associated with getting in shape become the good habits of exercise and eating right that support ongoing health and vitality. Health and vitality are associated with resilience and overcoming challenges and obstacles in life. See how that works?

Each of the dimensions can and does bear similar benefits in our life. Physical, mental, emotional, and spiritual dimensions uniquely insulate against trauma and challenge, as well as build resiliency; encouraging confidence and thriving. As each goal is achieved, then transformed into new good habits, we then create new goals. Again and again, as we reach closer to a beautiful life that is more fully under our control and less dependent on responding to random chaos of the universe.

CHAPTER 17

Homegrown is Best

> *"The glory of gardening: hands in the dirt, head in the sun, heart with nature. To nurture a garden is to feed not just on the body, but the soul."* **Alfred Austin**

Nothing compares to homegrown. Vegetables, flowers, grass, bushes, and trees combine to create an environment that is pleasing and satisfying. Communing with nature feeds the soul. One of my passions is gardening. As a kid I hated the weekly drudgery of weekend chores such as raking leaves and pulling weeds. Now as an adult, I find peace and serenity in my gardening chores. It is one of the strategies I most frequently use to process and deal with issues in my life, a kind of walking meditation.

There is nothing like the taste of your own grown vegetables and fruits. Sure the flavor is more intense but also the feeling of manifesting pure food out of a few seeds, dirt, and some water. You are witness to the natural phenomenon of plants turning trace minerals and sunlight into food. And you are being naturally defiant to the corporate food conveyance.

Food is a primary reinforcer. Primary reinforcers such as: food, water, and pleasure can be given or withheld as part of a behavioral shaping strategy. A food treat for a dog is a primary reinforcer to encourage specific behaviors such as sit, stay, or roll over.

The point I am making is that throughout our lives, most of us live under those in power, they control our food distribution. Parents to children, stores to customers, farmers to stores, corporations to the farmers, the control is mostly outside of us.

We work jobs and earn money to exchange for food to feel like we have some control. But as we are often made aware, the corporations, farmers, and stores have far more control of our food than we do. They control the pesticides, fertilizers, harvests, shipping, processing, packaging, and marketing of our food. For the most part, we find this all a fair trade because how many of us can really be full time farmers? There is a lot of work involved to create a harvest, but we can get involved even if that means we have one small tomato plant on our windowsill.

In childhood, we are in awe of our parents, as they can physically pick us up, drive cars, make life altering decisions, and most amazing of all, provide us with food. We behave in accordance with the rules in hopes of getting something delicious for desert! But as we grow older we begin to understand that we can feed ourselves. This reduces the parent's power over us. Sure they still buy the food, but now in our teens, we can declare, "I won't eat that," with more authority. We can become vegetarian or vegan if we wish. We can earn our own money and buy our own junk food at fast food places. Eventually we move out to our own apartment and do the shopping for ourselves. This is a developmental process that takes us from dependence to independence. And it feels good.

It is funny how the first harvest from my garden each year feels the same way. To know that my head of broccoli steaming in the pot was grown, watered, weeded, fertilized, cared for, and harvested by me just minutes before, it is so profoundly satisfying. It feels like I am an operator in the machine of life, not a victim of circumstances. I am a creator. Oh, and it tastes sooo good!

So much of our lives, are spent in pursuit of getting stuff. We focus almost entirely on consuming, our waking hours filled with efforts to support more and more consumption. How often do we actually create? Being productive is a need deep inside each one of us. Humans, who are thriving, are being productive. They produce something that has value. When you can produce something that has value, you step outside of the consumption hamster wheel and begin to feel the empowerment of creativity.

One of the great pleasures of home ownership is the power to do what you wish with your own property. Creating a garden is a fundamental right. But there are others who do not or cannot own their own home. How can they garden? So many ways, firstly there are community gardens in almost every major city.

Humans have transformed trash strewn empty lots into vibrant gardens filled with flowers and vegetables, and enriched the community and their lives. For those who only want to participate one plant at a time, I suggest a tomato plant or strawberry pot on the windowsill. Grow something and be proud.

Not everyone has the time to invest in a huge garden, but everyone has the time to invest in himself or herself. Working with the soil, even a mini garden in your window, has lasting and profound benefits that go deep to your soul. We are in charge even if for just that one moment. The courage to thrive takes a journey of many turns.

Everywhere you look is an opportunity to be the architect of your own destiny. Plant some seeds and watch them grow. Johnny Appleseed wandered the countryside flinging seeds everywhere as a kind of botanical graffiti. What if you sprinkled some wild flower seeds on an empty patch of dirt?

New research published recently in Neuroscience and Ecology indicates that contact and ingestion of healthy, friendly bacteria in soil can be even more effective than popular antidepressants! Eating fruits and vegetables grown from rich soil will make you happy. And isn't that what thriving is all about? To be in direct control of our happiness and having mechanisms to do so.

CHAPTER 18

Managing Anger

> *"Anger is an acid which can do more harm to the vessel in which it is stored than to anything to which it is poured."* **Mark Twain**

Yelling is not appropriate. And it does not accomplish what we think it accomplishes. As children, our yelling doesn't change the minds of our siblings or peers, and an adult usually has to intervene to settle matters. Yelling at a parent is almost always a pretty bad idea. Yelling at students does the opposite of commanding respect; it fosters disdain. Yelling at our business associates or employees brings only fear and power differentials, not cooperation. Yelling at your spouse, is a good way to live a miserable married life or get a divorce.

Thrivers seem to be able to acknowledge their anger and frustration without resorting to vocal power to win an argument. Yelling is only one manifestation of our anger. But it is the most often used and immediately damaging to relationships. It shows a lack of control.

Anger is not always recognized as a problem until the explosion occurs. Little bits of vented frustration would seem to solve the problem but that strategy is rarely is effective. Yelling is aggressive and about power. The recipient of that venting of anger usually has an immediate primitive defensive response. When that person is being defensive, the rage continues. Co-operation should be the goal rather than forced change and dominance.

When I was growing up, our home was filled with screaming and yelling. Kids fighting with each other, parents reprimanding, and parents punishing frequently. I vowed to myself that when I grew up and had my own home, there would be no yelling.

Meeting the woman of my dreams, my wife, Mary, I was finally on the threshold of fulfilling my dream of a loving home and family. Early on in our courtship, I brought up my childhood filled with yelling, anger, hurt feelings, and violence. She agreed that our home should be *Sanctuary*, a safe place to come to at the end of the day.

The world is dangerous and predatory, they try to steal your parking space, take your money, and cut you off on the freeway. Bosses are demanding, and often less than cordial in their commands. The journey home at the end of the day should be pleasant, with the anticipation of safety, smiles, love, and affection. We should be able to arrive home to *Sanctuary*.

A tradition at our home is to eat family dinner. One particular evening, I asked my son, Devin, to turn off the television and come to the dinner table. No response. Elevating my voice a bit, because he obviously didn't hear me, I emphasized, "Devin! Turn off the TV and come to table!" Still no response.

I now assume he was intentionally ignoring me and hey, wasn't I the boss around here? So I shouted: "DEVIN! TV OFF! COME TO TABLE, NOW!!!" He turns to me and asks; "Why are you always yelling at me?" Me? Yelling? I'm a psychologist, I don't yell, I thought to myself. And yet, I had to acknowledge that my communication strategy was not working.

The next evening, the same scenario was about to be played out. As dinner was put on the table I asked Devin, in the most normal voice I could muster, to turn off the television and come to the dinner table. As usual, he appeared to not hear me, and just as I was about to raise my voice, I remembered his admonishment about yelling. So I positioned myself between him and the television, got down on my hands and knees so as to be eyeball to eyeball with him, and in a soft, friendly, whispered voice said, "*Devin, turn off the television and come to the dinner table.*" He looked at me kind of surprised and asked, "Why are you whispering, Dad?" "*Because you told me not to yell!*" I smiled. Devin's face was confused and a bit scared, and he said, "Well can you quit it, because you are kind of freaking me out!" If you want to capture attention, whisper.

The communication between my son and I changed, therefore, action ensued. By eliminating the strategy of yelling, I was forced to be more creative. The catalyst for change wasn't the whispering per se, it was the capturing of his attention. So in the instance of redirecting a child from a preferred activity, it was up to me to first capture his attention and not assume that he will respond. I had to take ownership of my yelling as venting frustration and anger. Yelling taught my son nothing. However, the change in communication strategy allowed me to let go of the interaction as a power struggle and recognize the teachable moment for both of us.

While working with families in crisis, I mentally invented a device to help families with yelling and communication problems. It starts with the premise that yelling is about power, not communication of ideas. The family must agree to this premise and make a vow to focus on conveyance of ideas and directions rather than power and dominance. The device was to be shaped like a small traffic signal light pole about ten inches tall.

Affectionately dubbed, the Argument Buster 3000, it was a decibel meter that indicated normal conversation (green), elevated intensity (yellow), and yelling or shouting (red). The instructions would be to keep the conversation in the green while acknowledging the yellow moments and calm down. If the signal got to red, it would give an additional audible screech to end the yelling. If the device reached this critical level, then the participants were to walk away and calm down with self-soothing strategies.

By using this type of device, we can see behavioral conditioning to a more appropriate style. I still haven't given up on the device but now I am working on a cell phone app that would do the same thing. The point being that we sometimes need an external reminder or feedback to bring our attention to the problem. It is difficult because most of us feel quite justified in our behavioral choices. Self-control must be practiced to be mastered.

I remember learning the difference between commanding and demanding respect from my high school English teacher, Fredrick W. Funk III. My first day of class was the middle of the school year. I was apprehensive and trying to figure out the social structure at my new school. In walks in Mr. Funk, looking very much unlike any teacher I'd ever seen. He wore

Levi's, cowboy boots, colorful flannel shirt, and a denim cowboy hat. He presented, at least initially as a laid-back hippie. Although his full name was written on the board, he announced that we should simply call him Fred. I thought, this is going to be an easy class. How wrong I was.

He stood at the front of the class and patiently waited for the students to come to attention. Typical of any classroom, the students were talking amongst themselves and goofing off. Shortly, as the students became aware of his presence, they all quieted down and faced Mr. Funk. He asked, "Are you ready to learn? Good." And began teaching the class. Every time the class would devolve into talking and not paying attention, Mr. Funk would simply turn and face the class patiently waiting until order was restored. No yelling was required, ever.

Mr. Funk was the academically hardest teacher I'd ever had. He insisted that we learn. And he held us accountable, not by yelling or power, but simply by expecting excellence. This man commanded respect, rather than demand it. He carried himself with such assurance and self-dignity that we were embarrassed to misbehave. As it turns out he rarely had to resort to sending a student out of the class.

Fred's most devastating admonishment to me was to tell me he was disappointed. And on the other side, his most heart-warming praise was to tell me he was proud of my effort or accomplishment. He remains one of the greatest teachers in my life. His lessons persist through the years and go way beyond grammar and punctuation. He taught me that the volume of your voice is not equal to the strength of your argument.

Whether it's with children, in family matters, with co-workers in business, or any interpersonal communication, yelling tells others that you're out of control. They lose respect for you. Throughout every area of life, control of your anger through control of your voice commands respect. Demanding it with volume is a waste of time. Like in a family, the leader in a company gets more done by exuding confidence with firmness without yelling. Be secure enough within your core self to project a sense of inner peace and confidence.

It takes courage to change the way we do things. It takes courage to go out of our comfort zone and try new strategies. It takes courage to thrive.

CHAPTER 19

Meditation

> *"Just as you wouldn't leave the house without taking a shower, you shouldn't start the day without at least 10 minutes of sacred practice: prayer, meditation, inspirational reading."* **Marianne Williamson**
>
> *"Half an hour's meditation each day is essential, except when you are busy. Then a full hour is needed."* **Saint Francis de Sales**

Come on and give it a try. All the cool kids are doing it! Most people think of meditation as some wildly esoteric practice that is complicated, requiring an immense investment before some semblance of peace can be achieved. They think that one must twist their legs into the seemingly impossible pretzel called the lotus position and chant some magical incantations. The truth is far simpler and yet deeply profound in its ability to produce positive effect in our lives.

People who thrive report that they take time each day to reflect, contemplate, clear their mind, and breathe deeply. Benefits include a deeper sense of well-being, increased focus, decreased stress, improved vitality, and an appreciation for the pleasures of life.

The simplest form of meditation is simple drawing one's attention to the breath. Breathing with attention and intention has the effect of building the skill of focus and it is very peaceful. While there are many forms of meditation, one simply needs to take a few moments to be quiet and with one's own thoughts and then let them go. Start by sitting comfortably, closing your eyes, and drawing attention to your breath. Breathe out until empty and slowly inhale to completely fill your lungs. Pause at the top of your breath and then slowly exhale in a calm relaxed manner, staying focused on the sensation of the moving air. This will allow you to find a few moments of peace each day.

The benefits of meditation are so well researched and documented that I need not attempt to sell you on the idea. It is pretty easy to do a Google search and find all the research you need to be motivated. I would like to share some of the latest findings that excite me in this field.

During meditation, we find that the mind enters a very specific and observable state of altered consciousness. When we observe the brain with an *electroencephalogram* or EEG (that is the funny shower cap thingie with all the wires coming out of it), we find distinctive patterns emerge depending on the state of mind. The following states of consciousness are observed and categorized by the brain wave that predominates during that state of mind.

Alpha = Quiet restfulness

Beta = Active mind, fully awake, thinking

Delta = Deep sleep (stage 4) or unconsciousness, anesthesia

Gamma = Associated with creativity and inspiration during wakefulness

Theta = Rapid eye movement or REM sleep, dreaming

Theta waves are thought to be associated with the most restorative portion of our sleep cycle and, not coincidentally, theta waves are also seen in other altered states of consciousness like hypnosis, deep prayer, and meditation. This last piece of information is the most exciting to me.

REM sleep, where theta waves predominate, is the most restorative portion of our sleep cycle, then entering this state of mind voluntarily through meditation would increase the amount of time spent in that theta wave restorative/healing state of mind. Because entering this state is voluntary, it serves as a reminder that we are capable of being in control of our own healing mind.

The breathing technique described earlier can be taken further to enter this theta wave state of consciousness. Begin again by slowly consciously breathing. However, this time, extend each breath as long as possible, and make sure to breathe from the belly. This involves using the diaphragm rather than chest breathing. If you place your hand above your navel, you should feel the belling rising and falling, that way you know you are doing it correctly.

One can imagine making a game of trying to see how long you can extend one full cycle of in and out. The first try usually produces a result of an inhale/exhale cycle of about thirty seconds. Try to see how long you can comfortably extend that time. I find that after a few minutes of practice that I can get each inhale/exhale cycle to last about one and half minutes.

The next step is to count the slow, deep breaths and stay focused on the number of that breath. Count nine breaths and repeat two or three times. You'll be amazed at the feeling of entering your altered state of consciousness and the feelings of well-being that are created. As you can see, meditation does not have to be only for those who dedicate a great portion of their lives to a monastic lifestyle. It is attainable by all. This next story illustrates how I learned that meditation can be employed in many situations.

One fine sunny day I had the pleasure of visiting a beautiful Japanese garden that was open to the public. You know the kind, manicured plants and a *lake* of gravel raked into intricate designs and patterns. Through the middle of this lake was a low wooden walkway that resembles a pier or dock. At the end was a lovely open Pagoda with a beautifully ornate roof supported by four posts. In the middle was a long bench for sitting and contemplating.

Upon the bench, sat a Zen monk in the perfect meditation pose. He sat cross-legged, dressed in saffron robes, with a shaved head, and a serene peacefulness across his face. He was breathing ever so gently so that one would think he was a carved statue. Not wanting to disturb his meditation perfection, I ambled on until I spotted another monk in similar attire but his robes were considerably more faded, worn, and frayed at the edges.

This monk was bent over on his knees in the gravel with a wicker or reed basket at his elbow. As I drew closer I noticed that he was picking pine needles from the gravel and placing them in the basket. In my ignorance, I assumed he was a gardener and therefore quite approachable.

"Excuse me," I asked. "May I ask you a question about the garden?" "Certainly," was his slightly startled reply. "Why is it that you plant the pine trees so closely to the gravel lake? It would seem better to plant them further back to avoid having to pick the needles out of the patterns in the gravel."

The monk smiled gently and asked if I could see the monk sitting in meditation under the Pagoda. Yes, I could. "Who would you think is at more perfect peace, he or I?" he asked. It took me a few thickheaded moments but I realized they were equal.

Picking pine needles and sitting in silence are equally meditative. Cleaning and caring for the garden can be a path to enlightenment just as the structured breathing and quest for the Zen concept of Mushin or *no mind*. The state of mushin or no mind may take years of practice and is indeed a worthy goal. But for our purposes to get started in meditation, and achieve benefits quickly, we can stay focused on less intimidating practices.

One of the easiest quick meditations that I teach my clients is the *shoulder hunch reset*. When tension arises, it is most common for our chest muscles to become tighter. This causes our shoulders to tense as well and pull forward. This simple exercise will reset our attitude, mind, and body.

Become conscious of your shoulders and while breathing out slowly, feel them pull even farther forward and draw them up as if trying to touch your ears with your shoulders. Then rotate the shoulders back as you begin to breathe in and squeeze your shoulder blades together in your back. With your lungs now full, breathe out and relax with a letting go attitude. This resets your posture with the shoulders now aligned where they naturally should be which opens up the chest for easier and deeper breathing.

I like using the shoulder hunch reset several times each day. It is a quick easy technique that also reminds me to improve my posture. And the added oxygen to the brain can invigorate my thinking.

After shedding my addiction in my early twenties, I focused on martial arts training. This served as a kind of intensive outpatient treatment. One of the most important aspects of the art that I studied was mental focus and meditation. While I had dabbled in various types of mediation over the years, this structured approach seemed to work well for me. I have attributed much of my ability to overcome tragedy and trauma to my meditation exercises.

I would like to share a more complex meditation that which has its foundation in the simpler breathing exercises mentioned earlier. In Japanese, each of the fingers represents a different element. Chi (Earth) for the little or pinkie finger, Sui (Water) for the ring finger, Ka (Fire) for the middle finger, Fu (Air) for the index finger, and Ku (Spirit) for the thumb.

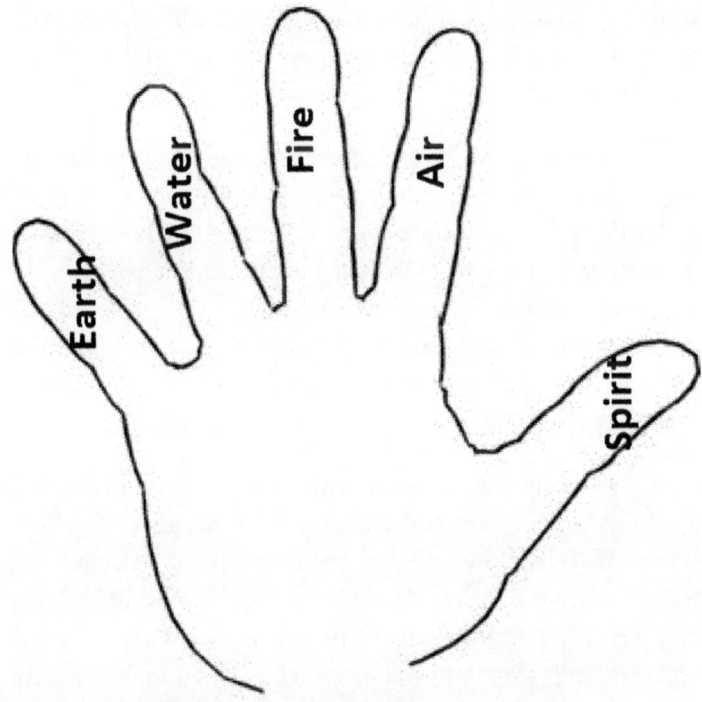

The meditation practice is to focus on one element at a time and breathe deeply and slowly, contemplating the essence of each element. The hands are placed on the lap, palms up, touching the tip of the finger to the tip of the thumb forming a circle. This symbolically connects each element in turn with the Spirit. The number of breaths can be simple, three for each element, or more complex, nine breaths for each element. As in the long version of deep breathing, take the time to see how long each breath can last.

So for the first element, Chi (Earth) palms up, tip of the little or pinkie finger touching the tip of the thumb. Center your thoughts on the essence of Earth and what it means to you. I like to think of grounding, the strength of the mountains, freshly tilled soil, and other images and thoughts that connect me with earth. Sometimes I just silently repeat the word Chi with each breath.

Second is Sui (Water), touching the tip of the ring finger to the tip of the thumb. Breathing slowly and deeply, centering the thoughts on the essence of Water. Here I like to think of water in its cycle from mist and vapor, to clouds, then rain and snow, streams then rivers, lakes and finally the ocean and the power of waves and the tide. Water represents the fluid and ever changing nature of the world and our lives. Adapting is required. Silently repeat the word Sui with each breath.

Thirdly is Ka (Fire), touching the tip of the middle finger to the tip of the thumb. Center your thoughts on the essence of Fire. Fire is the embodiment of change and transformation. Lightening, electricity, and the burning flame and physical manifestations of this element but also internal representations are our passions, laughter, even anger. Silently repeat the word Ka with each breath.

Lastly is Fu (Wind), touching the tip of the index finger to the tip of the thumb. Center your thoughts on the essence of Wind. We breathe the air, we feel the wind as is blows our hair and across our skin. The wind brings weather circling our planet in an endless cycle. The mind and its thoughts, the intellect, are represented by wind. Silently repeat the word Fu with each breath.

To finish: clasp your hands together and breathe gently and slowly in a very relaxed manner. The entire cycle of elements and breathing should leave you feeling balanced and clear. It should also provide for a very relaxed state of mind.

Personally, this is my favorite mediation, which I try to do at least once per day, usually in the early morning in my garden.

Meditation does not have to be intimidating. Too often, we are discouraged because a session or two does not provide immediate results. The deep inner peace, and confidence comes with much practice. As with anything, repetition makes it easier. Thriving is about investing in yourself. Meditation, whether it is in simple forms or more complex exercises, enhances life. The investment pays dividends that reach into every area of our life!

CHAPTER 20

Overreaction

"Nervous people tend to overreact." **Toba Beta**, *Master of Spirituality*

I tell teenagers that the way they react to a punishment from parents gets them in more trouble than the original crime itself. The control we show when we can take the pain of life speaks to our growing maturity and ability to understand the longer-term implications of our choices. Not being able to handle discomfort either physically, emotionally, or mentally, can cause us to take action out of proportion to what is our presenting situation. I will try to explain the oft used idiom "out of the frying pan and into the fire" to describe how when we are in pain or feeling discomfort that our choices will land us in a much worse place.

Out of the frying pan and into the fire, is similar to hating homework and then choosing to smoke pot to escape the mental frustration. Marijuana consumption is known to cause demotivation and yet generation after generation of teens seeks this escape which of course makes the problem even worse. Or a girl breaks up with a boy and said boy drives across town to profess his love in an overly dramatic way which proves to the girl how exceptionally needy and desperate he is. He has overreacted to the rejection, and behaved in such a way that makes the problem worse.

I have a story from my past that illustrates this particular problem, hopefully in a funny yet poignant way. Many years ago, a female cat of mine had a litter of kittens. Because of an upper respiratory infection, the kittens could not nurse from mother cat and had to be bottle fed by me. I decided that one of them was my favorite and named him Enlil, which is the name of the ancient Babylonian god of storms. I thought this was a fitting name for this little ball of fur, claws, and teeth.

When he was a little kitten, I found it was cute that he would harmlessly climb up my leg like a Tasmanian Devil, but as he got older, bigger, and stronger, it was less cute and far more painful. One day I was lazing on the couch watching a football game when out of the corner of my eye I could see Enlil stalking prey. After a moment I realized that the prey was my hand that was hanging off the couch and playing mindlessly with the tassel of the upholstery. Slowly he crept across the living room floor until at last he pounced. YEEOUCH!

With a supple leap he had landed cleanly on my arm and sank his claws and teeth deep into my flesh! My reaction? To jump up and yank my arm out of the jaws of this domesticated shark and scream my pain!

A cat's claws are shaped very similar to fish hooks and as my arm came away from the cat, the stripes of claw marks all down my arm were dripping with blood. What a painful mess.

I was so angry at the cat for doing this to me. For the next couple of weeks I had to explain to random people that yes indeed I was the victim of a vicious feline.

Sometime later, again lounging on the couch, playing mindlessly with the tassel, I relaxed watching another game. What else are Sunday's for? Again, I spied the terrorist feline stalking my hand from across the room. This time I planned to be smarter and faster than the vicious creature. Ah how ego can get the better of us.

Just as Enlil pounced, I yanked my hand away. This time the speed and timing were off just enough to cause great pain and discomfort and another shredding of the skin on my arm and hand. Dang! I was so angry at that darned cat. The pain of cat scratches is a unique pain. A piercing/burning pain that stings so intensely, that I was virtually incapable of logical thought. Ouchie, ouchie, ouchie!

My mind struggled to find a solution. I loved this cat but hated the pain he inflicted on me. He has so many other awesome qualities but I had to change his bloodthirsty habit or I was going to have to get rid of him. Of course eventually it occurred to me that this was a monster of my own making. But also, perhaps there was something I was doing that contributed to the problem.

There we were again. Same couch, same hand dangling off, same intensely focused hunter of a cat. This time I was determined to outwit him. As he launched through the air in a beautifully murderous arc, he landed on my arm. Claws and teeth felt like twenty pinpricks all at once. But this time, I resisted yanking my hand away. Sure it was initially painful, but slowly I lift each paw off my arm and the cat releases.

It seems this is the trick; to not over react to the pain. Part of living with such a domesticated killer is to deal with a bit of pain but if I refrain from over reacting, I can enjoy his company and not feel like a victim. I was causing the additional pain and destruction myself. I had to accept responsibility to control my actions and resist the urge to over react.

How many times in life do we feel like a victim of circumstance and walk away mentally, emotionally, and sometimes physically shredded and bloody? How much of that pain is due to our over reacting and causing most of the damage to ourselves by our actions?

Having the courage to thrive means learning from your mistakes. It means taking personal responsibility for how much our reactions contribute to the overall damage and pain. One can thrive in the face of pain. It is so much more difficult when we cause most of it ourselves and feel like a victim. The solutions to the problems of our lives are not external. The solutions must come from within. Thrivers know this and take responsibility for the solutions to their problems.

CHAPTER 21

Work Sucks

"Choose a job you love, and you will never work a day in your life."
Confucious

We need to change the focus of our efforts. Work implies something that we're obligated to do but don't really enjoy. Work at our job, work on our relationship, workout at the gym, etc. Work has become a word that demands our effort out of proportion to the reward. We resist work and only engage out of obligation or desperation.

The motivation to work seems to come from the accumulation of pain and avoidance of discomfort. We plan and look forward to the day when we can retire from work, settle into our relationship, and give up the battle against the bulge and just sit on the couch. This attitude results a major problem in that we give up the chance for being meaningfully productive, to be ecstatic and sweet in our love, and the health and vitality that comes from being active.

It's been said that a successful person wakes up and does exactly what they wish to do that day. If you love what you do, then you never work a day in your life. All too often, we just go to work and grind it out. Again the quote from Henry David Thoreau rises in my mind, "*A mass of men leading lives of quiet desperation.*" How sad. This is why so many people hate Mondays!

Growing up in Catholic school the nuns would often ask us if we heard God calling us to something called *Vocations*. In that context it meant being called to become a priest or nun. When I research the word vocation, it comes from the Latin root, Vocare which means to call. So when we use the word vocation in place of our profession or job name, and we enjoy being engaged in our vocation, we are pursuing our calling. If your job was indeed your calling, then it wouldn't be work, would it?

There are some professions, which appear to be more fun than others. Jobs that seem to have an enjoyment built right in. For instance entertainers, and artists, also athletes all give the impression of making a living doing something that they love or is their passion. Not all of us get to be an astronaut or a ballerina. Most humans work at a job that just pays the bills.

Perhaps we could develop a strategy of digging deep to find our passion and pursue that instead of just a job to get by. Or we might engage in Eckhart Tolle's the Power of Now and engage in mindfulness even at the mundane tasks and find enjoyment in a job well done. Sometimes the attitude is all that needs in order to change perspective.

We're told time and again by therapists and relationship experts that we need to work on our relationship. There's that dreaded word again, work. This instantly brings up resistance in one or both persons in a couple. Shouldn't coupling be fun? Of course there are cases where the matched pair are not good for each other and the foundation was suspect from the beginning. This happens when we don't do our due diligence at the beginning of the relationship. But for most people, the relationship can be resurrected or enhanced, not by working but by playing.

We should play in our relationship. Laugh more, smile more, be silly more. Learn about each other, make a game out of being clever and finding ways to excite each other. Doesn't that sound a lot more enjoyable than working on your relationship?

Invest in your relationship. One could be less enthusiastic about playing or being silly, so another strategy would be to think of romantic gestures and improving the relationship as an investment in content. Each act of kindness and togetherness bonds us and insures stability. Now that's what I call a long-term healthy investment I can get behind, certainly not *work*.

So sad to me that recess was my favorite subject in school, and now I have to go workout at the gym. When I was a kid, my brother and I would be sitting around and then get a phone call from one of our friends. He would ask us to come over to go swimming at his house. Riding our bikes the five or six miles seemed like nothing, in fact it was a lot of fun. Then we would go swimming most of the afternoon, then a neighbor would come over and have the great idea to play some football in the front yard. As the day wore on we would have to get home by the time the street lights came on, so my brother and I would race each other home for dinner. Nowadays that much activity would be called a Triathlon! Back then, we just called it Saturday.

We dutifully go to the gym and brag about how many minutes we can do on the elliptical machine or the treadmill, but are we really enjoying ourselves or just trying to convince others we are having a good time? We simply must stop calling it a workout and start playing more. Instead of the treadmill, how about hula hooping? I do see some positive change recently. Like instead of aerobics classes we know have Zumba dance class! That sounds like fun. To keep fit and in shape, find something that you love to do and most likely you will stick with it.

People who thrive engage life very deliberately. They use words to motivate and inspire the kind of action and choices, which support their thriving lifestyle. One could make the case that we're merely arguing with semantics over the meanings of specific words. However, it's clear that in order to thrive, we must do things and think things that cause us to take action that's supportive of our stated desires. Let's let go of the negative word *work* and replace it with these other concepts of vocation, playing, investing.

Thriving takes courage, it takes the courage to do something different and to embrace the change. It also takes courage to put the effort into change we are avoiding. There are so many things in life that don't come easily, and for some reason these things are not evenly distributed.

For example: when I go to the gym and utilize a session with a personal trainer, he asks many questions about workout habits and favorite exercises. My trainer asked me what body part or exercise did I avoid or least enjoy? He smiled and then put me through hell while focusing on the very areas I told him I didn't like!

A good trainer does this because he knows that these areas of weakness will show the greatest potential for rapid improvement. Also, by avoiding certain muscle groups, one can become unbalanced and prone to injury. Only doing chest and arms and avoiding leg day will not make for a balance person. Never skip leg day.

At the gym, and in life, we should probably have the courage to put the effort into the area we are avoiding. Go for what we dislike as we are probably avoiding it. This can be a wonderful, life-long self-improvement strategy. The socially avoidant should work on social skills. The socially focused person should learn how to be quiet and with themselves. Especially in therapy, this is where people often will avoid the most important thing they need to work on.

Have the courage to share with your coach, mentor, or therapist the deepest of secrets that you are avoiding. To continue to thrive we must acknowledge our weakness and vow to improve. Denial of our weakness only leads to shame and more weakness. It takes a great deal of courage but the rewards are so satisfying. We must face our obligations and face our fears. Courage is indeed facing our fears and obligations with grace and dignity.

CHAPTER 22

Black Belt Test

"A black belt is nothing more than a belt that goes around your waist. Being a black belt is a state of mind and attitude." **Rick English**

I've been asked many times about how I escaped the slavery of addiction. I give great credit to my participation in martial arts as a huge part of my salvation and recovery from drug abuse. That stage of my life, in retrospect, was my intensive outpatient therapy. Escaping the self-imposed tyranny of drug abuse was profoundly difficult and most people utilize some form of organized treatment.

I had always been a rebel and decided I needed to do it on my own. Little did I know how difficult that task would be. When I made the decision to quit drugs, I couldn't afford a treatment program, and I didn't find the sober meetings that I attended to be motivational. In fact, I found them downright depressing. Having the goal of getting a black belt would keep me focused on something transformational.

Another factor in joining a dojo or school to train in was to try to find a slice of happiness, which was difficult being so close to the time of my brother's death. Training in martial arts would keep me connected to him because, as kids he and I had been obsessed with Bruce Lee and Chuck Norris martial art movies. We would practice in our backyard the moves we saw on TV and in the movies.

It occurred to me that now was a perfect time to pursue this dream and achieve a profound goal. My goal was to learn the skills of self-defense to never being afraid again. And at the same time fulfill a lifelong dream that keeps me connected to my brother.

I began studying the Japanese martial art called Ninpo. My reason for joining this school was initially so that I could gain the skills to defend myself masterfully and no longer live in fear that someone would beat me up. More importantly for my needs, this school had a deeply spiritual component that supported personal mastery.

Being from a rough neighborhood, and being the only kids on our block to go to Catholic school, we were routinely picked on and bullied by older kids. My brother and I got into many fights with bullies.

I won a few of those fights, but mostly I got beat up pretty regularly by the bigger kids, in large part because I was very small for my age. Even after growing to six feet tall in high school, I never really felt big or even average. I always felt small and vulnerable. Hating this feeling propelled me to dedicate myself to study until I got my black belt.

This tale is told in two parts as my black belt test had two very distinct trials culminating in a greater degree of understanding and an ability to thrive. I dedicated many hours each week going to the dojo sometimes as many as six days a week. I progressed fairly quickly, mostly because of my physical background in boxing, gymnastics, skateboarding, and growing up in a tough neighborhood. Having body awareness, athletic ability, and a willingness to fight gave me an advantage.

I trained with this intensity for over two years, and in the process, purged my pain and anger. The mental aspects proved to be more powerful than the physical. In return I gained physical skill and peace of mind. Leaving the world of addiction behind became easier and easier. This regime also kept me responsible by being surrounded by other students who were focused on positive growth and development. It was an enriching experience in every aspect.

Finally had come the moment I'd dreamed of, to be able to test for my black belt! The test in this school was a unique affair that went far beyond simply performing an elaborate dance of memorized kata (forms or moves). All the students lined up in two parallel lines facing each other with white belts on one end rising in rank until reaching the black belts at the other end and our Sensei (teacher) at the far end with a Samurai sword.

The procedure explained to me, I was to slowly make my way down this two-line gauntlet of students, each throwing one punch, kick, lock, or throw as I defended each attack. This allowed me the opportunity to respond to spontaneous attacks as well as increase the difficulty as the line progressed to more difficult techniques. The test culminated with the Sensei drawing his sword and making a very deliberate attacking cut that must be avoided and then disarm the Sensei!

With a mixture of excitement and anxiety, I approached the line and began my trial. One by one I easily handled the white belts, moving through the intermediate ranks with skill and determination. Getting through the higher ranked students proved to be more difficult than I thought and was quite draining, and I caught a few painful punches but able to best each of my opponents and finally faced the Sensei. He drew his sword with a lateral cut intended to split me in two at the waist, however, I felt his intention before his draw and gracefully dropped below the cut and rose immediately body to body, and removed the sword from his hands. I passed! Oh the joy. The feeling of relief and excitement raced through my veins!

Something about a graduation always brings that accomplishment to the front of our minds. It raises the ego but also raises our self-esteem. By goal setting and working through all the levels of frustration and hard work, we come to accomplish a task that can never be denied. Our attainment of our goals fuels the deep down self-esteem that we are capable, if we put our minds to a task.

My mind went back to a time of addiction, a time when I felt helpless and weak. Now I felt that I had conquered my demon of feeling weak. Addiction was vanquished. Yet, something was missing. Although I had passed my black belt test, there was a lingering doubt, surely fueled by my poor self-esteem, that somehow I didn't really pass the test. Although difficult, it seemed to me that it should have been even more difficult.

The praise of my Sensei and the congratulations of my fellow martial arts students filled my ego, but that kind of praise quickly fades. The ego is very easily deflated. It takes something else to build the self-esteem. Of course my accomplishment improved my self-esteem somewhat, however, it was less satisfying than I thought it would be. The second part of this tale was even more interesting.

A couple of months had passed and I was on a trip to Northern California to visit my best friend from high school. Will was a capable man who took no crap from anybody and had a presence that told most people to avoid conflict. However, he was, and is one of the funniest people I know, being very quick to laugh and be joyful.

We decided to go out with our girlfriends to a local hotspot to play pool and listen to music. As we arrived, we noticed the parking lot to be very full. At the door, we were told by the fire marshal that the place had exceeded its occupancy limit. (You know those signs on the wall that says "Max Occupancy = 250") I had never actually seen this enforced. We were indeed annoyed but agreed to move on to another place less crowded. As we returned to our truck through the parking lot, in the dirt and dust we saw a commotion.

There in the middle of the dirt lot were two drunken fools pounding the crap out of each other in a scuffling fight. They appeared to know each other well and I surmised that they could be brothers, cousins, or best friends. And of course, fools. My look of disdain must have been obvious because just as we passed them one shouted to the other. "Did you see how that guy looked at us? Let's get 'im!"

Few things raise the hair on the back of your head like the shout, "Let's get 'im!" I wheeled around just in time to see these two beasts now coming after me at a full run. The next moments happened in a blur, but to me it also came down in very slow motion.

I immediately shifted thought process and assessed the situation, to get the lay of the land, preparing for what was to come. Open space in the parking lot, plenty of room for maneuvering I thought.

I took note of my best friend, Will, taking up a quiet observational position just out of my peripheral vision maybe eight steps away (I knew immediately that he was prepared to help me if needed but he was willing to give me my chance to deal with the situation). Will was not one to over react. It was very comforting and reassuring that he had my back. Also the girls were well out of harm's way.

Now the two men transformed into virtual attack dogs and were face to face with me, screaming obscenities in my face. Spittle flickered, with their venomous words of provocation. Daring me to take the first punch. I felt the rush of excitement that my chance had finally come! I could open up on them and be perfectly justified.

I looked them squarely in the eyes ready for battle. But other thoughts, more profound filled me in that moment. My deeper training in mental focus was kicking in. *Wait.* I had all the time in the world. I need not act first. Adjust to the situation as needed. Only move when it's called for. As I thought this, I became as calm as I'd ever been in deep meditation.

The calmer I became, and the more centered and peaceful I got, my demeanor must have changed, because the two fools slowly began backing up. Still filled with hate and provocation, they were demanding that I mix it up with them. "Throw the first punch! Come on wimp!" The more they screamed the calmer I became, fully confident I could handle any assault. My demeanor of calm confidence pushed them out of hitting range, them or me.

They clearly had changed their minds about this statue now smiling at them. They backed away until the nightclub bouncers ran out the back door because somebody informed them of what was going on in their parking lot.

As the bouncers arrived and grabbed a hold of the two fools (apparently they were well known fools) they renewed their verbal attacks safe in the knowledge that the bouncers would not let them go. The situation was now diffused. We had a hearty chuckle and headed out to the next pool hall down the road, a much quieter establishment.

Later on, discussing the events at our table with a couple of sodas, our girlfriends were talking excitedly about how I almost got beat up by these terrible ruffians. Will quietly got our attention and informed the girls that at no time was I ever in any real danger, in fact it was the fools who were in grave danger if things had escalated. "Stephen had this under control the whole time." He looked me squarely in the eye and said "Congratulations. You passed your real black belt test tonight."

My whole life, I had feared being weak. I feared being taken down and humiliated. I was now proud of being strong, but I had no need at all to prove it. Will was kind enough to see my transformation and point it out. He knew I could handle the situation and knew why it took greater strength to not throw a punch. Thank you very much my friend. That vote of confidence went straight to my core. No inflated ego, just a little growth in my self-esteem.

Training in martial arts proved to be one of the best choices in my life, to choose learning and personal mastery over addiction and chemical slavery. I would recommend the training to anyone, but any deeply invested endeavor will do. Overcoming our demons, accomplishing our goals, being tested by the real world, that's where the growth comes from, and the *courage* to *thrive*.

CHAPTER 23

Taking Down Time

> *"If a man insisted on always being serious, and never allowed himself a bit of fun and relaxation, he would go mad or become unstable without knowing it."* **Herodotus**

When I write about thriving, it sometimes can seem as if there is an urgency to be constantly productive. Constantly growing can be draining at times. We must balance our growth and motivation with time for recovery, rest, and reflection. In athletics, rest days are essential to muscle growth and repair. In art, there must be incubation periods, which allow the subconscious mind to fill again with creative content. It's good for the body, and good for the soul to take time off.

At the time I write this chapter, I've been battling a dreadful head cold. I didn't ask for this. I didn't volunteer to be a human petri dish, like a walking bacteria factory with the classy phlegm, mucus, and coughing. I am not allowed to get sick! I have much to do, many goals and aspirations. These things will not get done unless I do them.

I am not good at being sick, actually I am a pretty bad patient. Mostly because, I refuse to believe what my body is telling me and live in denial, which causes more harm. My habit is to try and tough it out, plowing through my day with all its responsibilities. This is not a good strategy because it doesn't give my body a chance to focus its attention on healing.

Of course, it's my wonderful wife who finally convinces me that I must slow down and take care of myself. In fact, she insists. Twice in my life, I have refused to believe I was sick. I flat out refused to slow down and take care of myself. My belief was that if I was going to feel like crud, I could to that lying down or being productive. This is an erroneous belief system and a very bad idea. Both times that I have done this resulted in coming down with walking pneumonia! Thank goodness for the miracle of antibiotics or I wouldn't be alive today.

With much reluctance I have rolled into bed and forced myself to be non-productive. I've taken care of my basic responsibilities, even accomplished a few small things. But for the most part, I've done not one bit of my usual thriving in the last week and a half. Instead, I've listened to my wife, and my body by mostly resting in bed. By giving my body the rest it needs in order to heal, I am hoping to avoid further degradation of my health and a speedy return to vitality.

One of my dreams was to someday run a marathon. 26.2 miles! (Accomplished March, 2013) Over the past few years I've made some halfhearted attempts to take on this challenge and begun a program of running. I've run quite a few 5K and 10K races. However, something would always come up that derailed my ultimate training goals.

Just when I thought I was in a fantastic training groove, this head cold hit hard and knocked me off my feet. I typically crave my morning runs. Lying in bed seemed like a luxury but all I kept thinking was that I was wasting valuable training time. It felt like my goals were getting further away.

When I tell my ego to take a rest, I realize that taking this downtime is not the end of the world, or the end of my training. It is a minor setback. So many people have set wonderful goals for each New Year, the resolutions are eager but as soon as they hit a wall, they use it as an excuse to give up.

We must NOT allow these minor setbacks to derail us from our goals. The courage to thrive means that even in the face of resistance, we dig deep and find the courage to continue our quest. Of course, that will have to wait until after my bowl of chicken soup and another nap.

Perhaps it would be better if I engineered more downtime. Scheduled time off to rest, relax, and reflect. It's not easy for me to take time off. By taking some downtime, we can recharge and be better prepared for the opportunities that are just down the road.

This has been a good time of reflection. Yes, I'm a victim of this dreaded cold bug. But I refuse to let it kill me. I will survive. My body's defenses are well equipped to wipe out this army of invaders, but I have to let them do it in their own time. Then and only then, will I charge forward with vigor in my quest to ever thrive.

Not all downtime is related to injury or sickness. A good life plan that focuses on balance includes downtime as a necessary part of thriving. Sleep is an important aspect of rejuvenation. While the deeper parts of sleep facilitate physical repair, the most restorative for the brain is the stage known as rapid eye movement or REM. This is the time of dreaming and without it, a person would go mad. When insomnia strikes or a bad night filled with tossing and turning, we feel not quite ourselves the next day.

The impressive speed of the cheetah is seen in explosive bursts. The cheetah cannot run for extended periods at full speed. It needs rest and rejuvenation. Humans are remarkable in their endurance as evidenced by our success as a species on this planet. But even we have our limits. Doing well over an entire lifetime requires careful consideration of our limits and working downtime into our thriving plan.

Take the time to have fun, to stop and smell the roses. Take the time to recognize when you need to recharge, recuperate, or repair yourself. Take the time to do silly and frivolous things once in a while. The exposure to different people, situations, and states of mind can be fuel for future creativity.

So many people in our culture aren't productive. They're sedentary and put forth very little effort. They're not creative but rather get by on the minimum required. Our reaction, as productive people, is to rebel against anything that would infer that we too fall into that category, even for a few moments or hours. Yet by doing so, we degrade ourselves to the point where sickness can take hold. Finding balance between productivity and downtime allows us to truly thrive.

CHAPTER 24

Hitting All the Red Lights

"Laughter and tears are both responses to frustration and exhaustion. I myself prefer to laugh, since there is less cleaning up to do afterward." **Kurt Vonnegut**

Ever have one of those days where you hit every single red light in town? I have recently had one of those *weeks*! A frustrating day is one thing but there are times where the endurance required to stay focused and optimistic is extreme.

The more effort I put in, the more resistance I got. My frustration level hit an all-time high, bringing with it negative fallout to my blood pressure and quality of life. When you find yourself in a place where every lane on the street you get into and every line you choose at the store, isn't moving, it might just be the universe telling you to slow down and reevaluate.

Its days like these, which cause me to believe that I couldn't even win a game of tic-tac-toe against myself!

When I was a young man, so many things had gone wrong in my life. I developed a belief that I had a reverse Midas touch. You may remember in the fable of King Midas that he was granted a wish that everything he touched be turned to gold. In my case, it seemed like everything I touched turned to crap.

Being in a state of belief that everything will turn to crap, becomes a self-fulfilling prophecy. The negativity turns in on itself, which is quite exhausting. If we are not careful, self-defeating thoughts can become a very nasty habit. It can also become a way of life. Pessimism insidiously eats away at the quality of our lives.

My experience has been that while we can get through these difficult times, the endurance of it can be quite draining. We need to feel that we have some control over our destiny, beyond just hoping that things will get better.

In the case of King Midas, he soon realized that if everything he touched turned to gold, he could never have food or enjoy relationships. It turned out to be a curse. If everything I touch turns to crap, then perhaps I can repurpose it as fertilizer for future growth!

Time to reevaluate. Slow down; take it easy, traffic will eventually ease up. Everything looks better after a good night's sleep. In the morning, spend some time crafting a plan on paper. A proven strategy is to list all your frustrations, responsibilities, and commitments. Take a good look at what's a drag on your personal resources and reprioritize. Allocation of your limited personal resources will mean that you have to say *no* to a few people. That's okay. In order to thrive in this world, we need to make sure we're not overextended.

Another strategy is to simply get off the road. Yes, avoid traffic lights altogether. For me, taking a long back-roads ride on my motorcycle is just the medicine to clear my head. Sure I have to stop for a few lights or stop signs now and then, but the majority of my ride, through the back roads of California, is wide open. I can go for miles and miles without hitting traffic, or stops. Enjoying the beauty of the countryside as I listen to the musical hum of the engine.

Certainly there are other ways of getting off your metaphorical highway. Turn off your computer, play board games with your family, take a walk on the beach or along the river, or stroll through a neighborhood park. Even just pure laughter at the absurdity of what we are facing can bring relief. Whatever your situation, if you find that you're hitting all the red lights, slow down, get off the road, reprioritize, and hope for a better night's sleep. Everything looks better in the morning.

Thriving is not a state of never having to stop at red lights or weather a storm. Thriving is strength and endurance despite the obstacles and storms. If you feel knocked down and put upon, then taking some time to slow down and change perspective can give you renewed energy for thriving tomorrow.

CHAPTER 25

Development of Relationships

"You are the average of the five people you spend the most time with."
Jim Rohn

People who thrive tend to be able to manage their friendships and relationships with grace and dignity. One of the ways in which they do this is by understanding each relationship in context. Each person interacted with is understood from the dimension of reality rather than what one wants the relationship to be. Thrivers manage deliberate friendships through thoughtful analysis of depth.

Most people are troubled by friendships and relationships because of what they want out of them rather than dealing with reality. Sometimes a person, no matter how wonderful they are, is simply an acquaintance rather than something deeper. Wanting the other person to fill a need in our emotional life rarely leads to satisfaction. Not everyone who we're friendly with meets our criteria for true friend. If we understand the context of the relationship, then we can manage our feelings and be content with reality.

Here we will explore human development of friendships as children, and then how we manage as adults. Throughout childhood it seems that friendships develop without much effort. At times we seem lucky to live next door to a kid our own age, or unlucky to have moved away from our friends, and have to begin again at the next school.

Developing friendships is a life-long task. All friendships have a developmental arc that spans from initial meeting, through to mature friendship status or dissolution. As humans we approach and deal with friendships differently throughout our lives. The most dramatic changes and obvious qualitative development happen during the journey through childhood to early adulthood.

Throughout childhood, friendships can be described in terms of *proximity, activity, interests*, and *values*. While we have individual friendships as well as group friendships, I will concentrate more on individual friendships, as they have more bearing on later development of relationships.

When we are small children, we label individuals as *friend* based on certain criteria. Our parents identify our friends as anyone about the same size and age as us, and we begin to use the word friend to mean those that are small and just learning language like us. So basically we develop friendships with those within our *proximity*. If a person is short and are near me, they must be my friend. This definition seems to remain mostly constant through kindergarten or first grade. Ask a kindergartener who his friends are and he will usually recite the entire attendance roster from his class!

Then in the early school years something happens. We begin to notice that some kids play different games and engage in different *activities*. It's at this stage that we generally consider a friend someone who engages in the same games or activities that we do.

Some kids play kickball, others play soccer, some play tetherball, while some hang out and socialize. We like to hang out with others who share our favorite activities. Someone to play with is indeed a friend. This is a shift from parallel play or playing in unison but not really interacting, true interactive play involves more social skills and shared perspective.

At the end of early school years and beginning of middle school, another change takes place, which adds to previous developmental definitions. We begin to seek to spend more time with those who have status, in addition to being near us and sharing activities.

Now we define friendships in terms of shared *interests*. These new friendships develop into groups or cliques. Status is very important. Popularity and being cool become more important than *proximity* and *activity*. The skaters hang with the skaters. The preppies hang with the preppies, etc. The type of music one listens to mean a great deal to others.

We surround ourselves with those that give positive feedback about our *interests*. This is the beginning of some serious social challenges. It is important to have the right friends. Old alliances of *proximity* and *activities* and even loyalty are seriously challenged. Many times a group or clique is developed or joined, simply because these people do not tease us. Acceptance is attractive when popularity doesn't win out. This is also the time that young people are at their greatest risk for peer pressure. A reputation begun and set during these years has long lasting effects. Aberrant or deviant behaviors often arise out of peer pressure such as drug use, delinquency, and emerging sexual behaviors.

In high school a new phenomenon begins, and is timed with the development of abstract reasoning skills. Friendships begin to be formed and strengthened by shared *values*. The previous definitions of friendships hold, but with the new added layer of values.

A teenager's job is to separate and individuate from his/her parents in order to begin developing an independent code or *value* system. The ability to choose and maintain friendships is an exercise in self-directed destiny, and a way of demonstrating what values an individual holds. This is a much more mature level of friendship development, precisely because it is not shallow.

Our *best* friend is often someone with whom we share similar values. We see young people going outside of their group or clique to form bonds of friendship, which previously would seem counter-intuitive because they may not raise social status. This level of maturity is not universal.

It is also true that the values shared or desired may in fact be negative. We notice that the kids who do drugs share that value. The kids who are bullies, share that value. The negative values are what most parents and society worry about when their child is striving for autonomy because we don't trust their judgment, often rightly so.

During our adolescent years we are so busy trying to meet school requirements, the demands of our parents, and getting invited to some social event, that we don't give much thought to our developing friendships. This leads to default friendships that are just a continuation of past relationships. They are largely maintained by loyalty and familiarity. Later we find out that loyalty is not the only reason to remain friends.

A new kid in school usually has a tough time because he has no such loyalties or familiarity. So he may resort to a previous level of development and try to form friends based on proximity (who is in his class), activity (those on the sports team or chess club), interests (music, politics, drugs), and lastly values (altruism, creativity, antidisestablishmentarianism!).

Many high school kids do maintain friendships solely based on *proximity* (they live next door to me), or *activity* (they are into sports), or *interests* (they like punk music). Some would say that many adults continue with the habit of forming and basing friendships for these reasons, and they may mature into friendships that share *values* (such as loyalty). But the most valued and fulfilling friendships or relationships are based on shared *values*.

In the development of adult friendships, we often try to gain companionship with someone because of their physical beauty, their social status, their access to resources, their personal magnetism, and even sometimes because we feel sorry for them.

I might initiate and maintain friendships with my neighbors (*proximity*), or with people at the gym (*activity*), or my acquaintances through the local renaissance faire (interests), but the most important friendships I have are with those that share the *values* that I hold dear for physical, mental, emotional and spiritual health.

The list of values that I and my dear friends share include sense of humor, respecting family, service to humanity, creativity, loyalty, fidelity, and intellectual honesty. Each person defines themselves in terms of values and, therefore, defines their true friends in terms of how they support and respect those values.

Romantic relationships also follow a developmental arc. Very few romantic relationships begin without some physical attraction, however, once in a deeply committed emotional attachment, physical beauty becomes less important than it once was.

There are many very good experts in the field of relationship theory, and I can only speak from my studies and experience. It's true that the initial rush of emotions that are the hallmark of romantic love definitely fades over time. What sustains a romantic relationship is true friendship based on shared values. Understanding the attraction to humans in our lives will help us to successfully navigate these complex social relationships.

The most successful romantic relationships have several conditions that bring about long lasting joy and satisfaction. Firstly, having developed themselves as individuals they come to the relationship fully formed rather than deeply damaged seeking rescue from the other person. Secondly, they are compatible or cooperative with each of the friendship dimensions. And lastly, they learn to grow with each other throughout the course of their time together and the rest of life.

Friendships can be inclusive or exclusive. Inclusive friendships welcome newcomers and are usually accepting of individual differences. Exclusionary friendships are based on excluding others and not accepting of differences. In childhood friendships, we may feel negative about exclusive or exclusionary situations; but in adulthood, loving or romantic relationships should be exclusionary because in is more supportive of the family unit.

Through our friendships we gain support, social bonding, and so much more. Our capacity to handle frustration and sorrows goes up as we have and utilize our friendships in healthy ways.

Developing friendships and other relationships in perspective allows us to not have unrealistic expectations of what others should do to meet our needs. Relying on a person to complete us or fix us will most often lead to disappointment. Each of us is responsible for our own happiness.

I have friendships with many types of people in many areas of my life. Keeping them in perspective is a deliberate act. This act is crucial to being responsible for my own happiness, while allowing these social interactions to be nurturing and supportive.

We are social creatures indeed. We have a deeply rooted drive for acceptance by others and validation of our existence including shared experiences with like-minded humans. Thrivers do not rely on happenstance, but rather are deliberate, active participants in managing friendships.

CHAPTER 26

Do You Have Something on Your Soul?

"Character cannot be developed in ease and quiet. Only through experience of trial and suffering can the soul be strengthened, ambition inspired, and success achieved." **Helen Keller**

A friend and I were having a wonderful conversation about different anxiety causing issues, when she suddenly asked me, "do you have something on your soul?" A little taken aback I corrected her by asking if she meant to inquire what was on my mind. But no, she said it was a translation from her native Romanian.

Which got me to thinking that there is indeed a big difference between what's on our mind and what's on our soul. For the most part, I think, that we can divide the categories into the profound and the mundane. The philosopher, Mercia Eliade, described a similar difference between the sacred and the profane. Sacred meaning special, non-ordinary, and exalted, and profane as everything else that is ordinary. The differences between mundane and profound thoughts are a bit more complex.

When we ask, "Is there something on your mind?' or "Is there something on your soul?" We are asking two very different questions and of two very different parts of ourselves. The word *soul* is often connected to spirituality and religion. In our conversation today, let's simply let the soul refer to that part of each of us that's more than the sum of our material and physical parts. A place beyond our pumping heart and thinking mind, perhaps it's the seat of our core essence as a person.

When we ask someone "Is there something on your mind?" The answer can be as simple as "yes, I am thinking of a song I heard this morning," or "I'm trying to decide what to order for lunch." When we ask, "Is there something on your soul?" we are asking something much deeper.

We can have any combination of concerns that we stress about related to the mundane or ordinary world around us. Taxes, finances, travel plans, work issues, gardening tasks, emails to respond to, travel plans, conversations, tasks, etc. But what's on our soul are the personal and interpersonal imprints, questions, and dilemmas that we wrestle with, in order to hopefully, and eventually find some inner peace. We realize that the mundane tasks will always be there, but we hope and strive for resolution to the questions on our soul, which are often seen as existential dilemmas. Profound questions and concerns demand that a resolution be found in order to settle things.

What weighs on our soul are the interactions that mean something to us, whether it's about our own decisions about which way to go in life, or trying to interpret our relationships and the myriad of details that tell us the hidden story of our standing with each other. Big questions like: who am I, what am I doing with my life, what is the meaning of it all, does she love me, speak to the foundations of our lives, our purpose and meaning?

One of the defining features of what weighs on our soul is that the various life struggles often leave us feeling very alone, perhaps misunderstood, and a bit afraid of the outcomes. What weighs on our soul is often caused by the losses of our lives leading to utter loneliness. The lack of external human validation leaves us feeling like a shell of ourselves, very uncertain of our own qualities and value.

I am fond of saying "Your brain will focus on what you feed it." This implies that the pool of thought you choose to immerse yourself in will affect your continued and future thoughts. Positivity breeds positivity and negativity leads to more negativity. There is saying from Henry Ford, "If you think you can do a thing, or you think you can't, you're right." It's the thinking that makes it so. What you choose to dwell on can have a significant effect on your life.

When you ask yourself, "What is on my soul?" then you can embark on a personal journey of self-discovery and self-actualization. Each of us has the opportunity to commit to the challenge to not just merely survive in this life, but to make decisions and choices that leads you to truly thrive. When we ask others "what is on your soul?" we then know that we are asking something profound and perhaps we can be a catalyst for the other to find the answers to thrive.

CHAPTER 27

Your Mind Will Focus on What You Feed it

"We become what we think about all day long." RW Emerson

The human brain is a marvelously fantastic machine. It does things that even the most amazing supercomputers cannot do involving everyday tasks. They say that we only use about ten percent of our brains. This is simply not true. We use all of our brain but not all at once, and not all of it conscious. It can be argued that we consciously only use ten percent of our brains while the remaining ninety percent is subconscious. This subconscious mind is like a hyperactive child with no toys.

One of the easiest ways to see beyond the hidden veil of what our subconscious mind is doing is through the content of our dreams. For all of human existence, the dream world is the most mysterious and much effort has been put into the translation and understanding of our dreams. Both Sigmund Freud and Carl Jung, early pioneers in the field of psychology, were fascinated with dreams and wrote many books on the interpretation of those dreams.

Dream interpretation tells us what is being expressed by the subconscious through the language of symbols. Sometimes those symbols are exceptionally vague, and other times it is quite obvious what they mean. The subconscious mind is given a chance to play in our dreams. Much of what we encounter on a daily basis works our way into our dreams.

Another role of our subconscious mind is to attend to functions that do not necessitate conscious control such as: heart rate, blood pressure, tissue repair, daily balance, digestion, etc. These functions are regulated by what's called the parasympathetic nervous system.

Lastly, the main role of the subconscious mind is to assess the content of our sensory input and make sense of it. It analyzes the data to help us make future choices. In primitive times, this data collection and analysis helped us remember which foods were good to eat, migration patterns of game animals, and predicting behavior of our tribe mates.

In modern times, our powerful subconscious brain is crunching volumes of data that sometimes overwhelm the senses. As a species, we're often so overwhelmed that we seek escape through any means possible. This stress is responsible for a percentage of the drug/alcohol problem, as well as the various maladaptive behavioral or *process* addictions.

When I was about 13 years old, the video game Asteroids was very popular. Taking some of my earnings from my first job as a paperboy, I slugged dozens of quarters into the machine to try to beat the game. After several hours, I could not take any more and went home, *quarterless.*

That night, I tried desperately to close my eyes and sleep, but the game's visuals persisted each time my lids dropped. Finally I fell asleep but my dreams were filled with the game and the frustration of not winning.

When I awoke in the morning, my mother was shocked at the deep circles under my eyes and I felt even worse. My dreams of the game gave me no respite or relief. It was as if I hadn't slept at all. Several other times in my life I've done something similar. Haven't you? Think about it. Your brain will focus on what you feed it.

The good news is that a large part of the content we expose ourselves to is under our control. The engineer dreams of the solution on how to build a bridge, the musician dreams of music and a new song emerges, the scientist dreams of her work and innovative ways to take the next step, and the artist has visions that express the human condition. If we feed ourselves a steady diet of garbage television, well then, as the old saying goes, "Garbage in, garbage out!"

I have found that people who focus their daily efforts on seeing the positive side of life, find that positivity most often. Those that focus on the negativity and flaws in life, also find what they are looking for. You can bring your daily focus more under your conscious control by deliberately feeding yourself on the content of your desire.

I tend to read a great deal about personal growth and development, journals about the field of psychology, and positive forward thinking magazines about science and technology growth. Recently, I have begun tuning out my favorite crime drama television shows because the content of psychotic murderers and vicious psychopaths is not what I wish to dream about. Instead, I am tuning in to more art, history, and science programs. For some much needed non-thinking downtime, I watch comedy shows and the occasional reality TV program.

Careful consideration of the content and processes we go through each day can have dramatic effects on our overall well-being. The drug addict obsesses all their brainpower on procuring and consuming their drug of choice. In the recovery process, they are directed to spend much more of their time on personal growth and development, which has the positive effect of redirecting the attention away from the self-sabotage and triggers.

If we assume that self-actualization, reaching higher states of consciousness is the goal of personal growth, then we would do well to keep more conscious control of the feeding of content to our brain. Just like the body requires good caloric content to function optimally, the brain functions much better on content that supports the desired mental state. It seems so obvious, however, all too often a person will behave like a victim of circumstance and believe that they must focus on the drama and trauma. This is an erroneous belief that needs challenging.

Victim modality beliefs support the choices that keep us from thriving. If I think that I am indeed a victim, then the external world has all the control. I must plod along and take what is offered me or is within my immediate grasp. Challenging that belief frees us from the self-imposed tyranny but it takes a leap of faith and a changing of the mind to believe that I am the architect of my own destiny.

Taking charge of what you feed your brain is one of the most important steps to thriving. Surround yourself with content and influence that raise your level of life. Fill your mind with words of wisdom and encouragement. Acknowledge that you have choices in many areas of your life, and those choices can lead to thriving!

CHAPTER 28

Finding Inner Peace

"I get those fleeting, beautiful moments of inner peace and stillness – and then the other 23 hours and 45 minutes of the day, I'm trying to make it through this world." **Ellen DeGeneres**

The power of inner peace cannot be overstated. The sense of control is profoundly satisfying. I think of iconic figures, both fictional and in reality who display a supreme confidence that tells us they've found their inner peace. In cinema, characters played by John Wayne or Clint Eastwood come to mind. But also people such as Bruce Lee, the Dali Lama, Benjamin Franklin, Joan of Arc, or Maya Angelou give the impression of possessing inner peace and confidence.

What the external projection of confidence from these people conveys, comes from finding a deeper sense of self and peacefulness. Meditation, attention to a specific task or endeavor, serves to cultivate these feelings and conditions. For some it's gardening, pottery, knitting, woodworking, art, science, and even mathematics. All these things serve to focus the mind resulting in also finding the inner self-confidence.

Most people come to the practice of meditation seeking inner peace. The answer, we're told, lies in quieting the mind through mindful breathing and years of practice.

During my early martial arts training many years ago, I had the chance to train with Shoto Tanemura, the grandmaster of Genbukan Ninpo of Japan. He was visiting our dojo in Los Angeles and it was a privilege and honor to train with such an accomplished and masterful marital artist. At the end of the training session, we gathered to sip tea and hear wisdom as well as ask the sensei (teacher) questions about the history of the martial art or on certain techniques.

One by one sensei invited questions from each of us students. When it came time for my question, most of the good ones had already been asked. So it occurred to me to ask about my difficulties in mediation. I asked how to find or create a perfectly peaceful space for the meditation.

Each time I would attempt to meditate, something would distract me. I explained about the distractions of the dog barking, or telephone ringing, and the police siren in the distance. I went on further to tell him how I could even hear the clock ticking or the air conditioner blowing and all of these things prevented me from finding peace.

He listened politely until I was done, and then offered this little gem of wisdom. He took a deep slow breath and pointed his finger at my chest. "For you. You must practice slow breathing until you can find perfect peace on the center divider of the freeway," he admonished. Well, everyone chuckled at this. My lesson was that I had to accomplish the very thing I feared. My task was not to follow the easy path but to face the most difficult. And that would be to master my mind to free myself of distractions. A great lesson but somewhat disheartening because I knew this would take a very long time.

All through my life, I have meditated and struggled with distractions. Perseverance kept me going. Many of my accomplishments had given me a good measure of confidence. I had found joy in learning, satisfaction in my work, fullness in my heart from love, and measures of inner peace . . . but it still eluded me. Meditation was a challenge. Then I had the most extraordinary of circumstances. I ran a marathon.

The Los Angeles Marathon is held every year and is called the Stadium to the Sea race. It starts at Dodger Stadium in Chavez Ravine and winds through downtown LA, Hollywood, Beverly Hills, then out to the coast finishing at the Santa Monica Pier. In all it is 26.2 miles!

Having taken up running a few years previous, the heavy breathing had seemed quite meditative and I was enjoying the improvements in my athletic abilities. So I had decided to challenge myself to complete the entire marathon.

There I was at 7:00 AM in the Dodger stadium parking lot, which was the staging area for the start of the race. All through my training I had been focused on my heart rate to determine how much effort I was putting out.

As an example, most healthy adults have a resting heart rate of about 70-72 beats per minute. An athlete can have a much lower resting heart rate of 50 or even below! Mine was about 55 which is pretty darned good and represented years of training and many miles of sweat and worn out running shoes.

During a run, I would try for a target heart rate of about 160 beats per minute.

Back in the parking lot, about 15 minutes before the start of the race, about 26 thousand of my fellow runners and I were eager with anticipation. I was shocked to find my heart rate at 115 beats per minute just standing there waiting! With 26.2 miles ahead of me, I did not wish to waste any of my energy or inner fuel. I needed to calm down and find peace. With nothing to lose, I sat down in the middle of the crowd and began my slow, deep breathing.

The crowd of runners continued to speak to each other, the announcement speakers kept sharing their announcements, the motivational music continued, and I was able to ignore all of it. I didn't care what people thought of me, just slow deep breathing, finding my peaceful center. I follow a very specific breathing meditation with several mental milestones throughout, however, I really only spent about 6 minutes with my eyes closed sitting on the ground.

When I opened my eyes, I checked my heart rate, which came back down to 71. I had done it! Lowering my heart rate was a minor victory compared to the peace I felt despite all the distractions. It was in a parking lot rather than the center divider of the freeway, but a victory nonetheless.

What will be your path to inner peace? Not everyone finds it through meditation, although it's a very tried and true method. Perhaps your path is through prayer, or gardening, or walking in nature. The target is to find that place deep inside that is often hidden due to the urgency of the immediate demands of our environment. We need to be able to shut out the distractions, even for a few moments, in order to regain our center, our balance point, and self-control.

Never in my life did I believe that I would find perfect peace in the parking lot of Dodger stadium. How true my sensei's instructions would be. Since then I've been able to go back to that peaceful place in my mind and heart at will. Distractions no longer bother me.

I know what I seek and what it feels like. I would love to share that with you, but the truth is that you will have to find it for yourself. No matter how long it takes, the journey is yours to take. Never give up. Along the way you will also find many moments of peace, joy, and love. And that is truly *thriving*.

CHAPTER 29

Atonement

"I am not a saint, unless you think of a saint as a sinner that keeps on trying." **Nelson Mandela**

This chapter was written on one of my favorite Jewish holidays. Yom Kippur, the Day of Atonement, during which it is prescribed to fast (abstain from food) and contemplate one's sins and/or failures over the past year.

What a wonderful tradition of self-contemplation, and action with intent to mend one's relationship with God and our fellow humans. It would seem to be a real *thriving* move to not simply say *sorry* and move on, but instead continue to rectify any hurts, intentional or unintentional. I hope my humble attempt to explain this beautiful holiday is respectful, as I am by no means a Jewish scholar, merely a curious student of the religious ways of others.

Being raised Catholic, I was instructed to go to confession which involved telling the priest your sins, then sincerely being contrite, followed by penance. Penance is similar to atonement, but penance most often was a set of prayers to be repeated a certain number of times usually related to how severe or how numerous a person's confessed sins were. This ritual was to provide absolution for one's sins.

As kids, we would judge others as to their sinfulness based on how long it took them to say their penance in church after leaving the confessional! The problem with this system seemed to be that the atonement was only directed towards God rather than the injured party.

Making apologies and asking for forgiveness are empty and meaningless without atonement. When a person says, "I'm sorry," they mostly do so to get out of trouble or to be simple in placating the other wronged person. But that kind of apology is devoid of meaning, without an attempt to truly make up for one's mistake or error.

If I step on your foot and then offer a halfhearted apology, then you do not believe me, and you still have throbbing toes! You're diminished in your health because of my actions. However, if I were to truly attempt to atone for my mistake, I would also offer to perhaps buy you a pedicure or a foot massage! If I make a mistake and diminish you, then I feel it is my obligation to atone and repair the damage as best I can. That means leaving you in a better place than before I damaged you.

My great-grandfather used to say, "don't do anything you will later have to apologize for!" It's a great principal to live by. However, it's nearly impossible because we are, after all, human. Humans often fail, even with the best of intentions. But if we commit ourselves to a life of continual incremental improvement, then the incidents of having to apologize should become less frequent and certainly with lower levels of intensity.

Thriving in life is negatively affected by guilt. Guilt is a heavy burden, which can weigh us down. Atonement or penance can relieve oneself of the guilt and pave the way for the opportunities to thrive. Some people convince themselves they have nothing to be guilty about. This is a delusion of vanity.

All of us are imperfect and occasionally make mistakes, which hurt other people. Searching your own heart and being fearless in a personal moral inventory can have deeply profound positive effects. Dig deep, understand your failures, and make the commitment to improve. Living life deliberately rather than haphazardly results in a much higher quality of life.

We may or may not receive forgiveness from a person we have wronged. If we're truly sorry, and attempt to atone for our mistakes, then the only thing left is to forgive ourselves. Over the years we do two things, part of us gets emotionally hammered by our guilt and self-depreciation for our mistakes; the other part hardens our heart and distances us from other human beings.

That first part erodes our self-esteem, and the second part isolates our empathy and connectedness to our fellow human. The solution is in atonement, seeking forgiveness, admitting failure, but building oneself up through knowing we have put forth honest effort to become a better human being each day of our lives. This exercise frees us to *thrive*!

I know that my own journey has brought me to this place of being a teacher, a psychologist with a mission to help others. In the darker past of my youth, I hurt a great many people. I had thought my addiction would only hurt me, but the truth was that I left a path of wreckage along the way. I'll never know many of those I hurt and cannot atone or make amends to each of them. Part of why I became a psychologist was to pay it forward. By helping people in my professional life, I feel that atonement is at hand. I have a long way to go but it feels like thriving.

CHAPTER 30

Random Wisdom

> *"A single footstep will not make a path on the Earth, so a single thought will not make a pathway in the mind. To make a deep physical path, we walk again and again. To make a deep mental path, we must think over and over the kind of thoughts we wish to dominate our lives."* **Henry David Thoreau**

Not every thought deserves its own chapter. This seemed like a good place to jot down a few important points that have been helpful to me and many of my clients and students.

I Statements

If there were one life lesson you could teach your younger self, what would it be?

I have contemplated this question for many years. Thinking about what a young skull full of mush I was, the lesson would have to be simple and direct. This concept is immediately applicable to life. *Use I statements.*

The utilization of I statements is a concept of taking personal responsibility for one's own feelings. Saying, "I feel upset when ..." empowers the individual by taking responsibility for the feelings. This is a choice. The opposite is when we say, "He made me angry," or "She made me feel bad about myself." This is giving away your personal power to others who may wish us ill or simply control us.

As a child and teenager, I gave away my personal power so often that I had none left for myself. I blamed everyone and everything for my bad feelings. I was at the mercy of the world to make me feel good or bad. I had no control.

This left me feeling very much like a victim much of the time. It also set me up for feeling justified in making myself feel better with drugs. If life was so unfair and unkind, then I deserved some relief, and drugs provided that relief.

When I got clean from drugs, I was forced to face my responsibilities. I had to take ownership of my role in causing much of my own bad fortune. I learned the skill of using I statements when I began personal psychotherapy.

From then on, I would acknowledge my role in any trouble and take ownership of my feelings. This was very powerful. While random misfortunes would continue to happen and occasionally people would attempt to make me angry, I now had the choice in how I would feel in response to the stimulation. That is taking back your power!

Practice using I statements often, you'll be surprised how good it feels. I wish someone had taught me that skill in high school, or even earlier.

Death of Fairness

"It's not fair!" This is the shout of every child when faced with the reality of life. We humans invented the concept of fairness as if it was an absolute that existed in the universe, independent from humans and our observations.

The human-made illusion of fairness gives us an unattainable goal, and yet somehow seems reasonable. We cannot reconcile living in a universe without a concept of fairness because the world itself is so unequal in its distribution of pain or pleasure. We reasoned that there must be balance to offset our pain and misfortune.

Our sense of justice arises out of the concept of fairness. We developed laws to help right the wrongs we do to each other. Siblings appeal to their parents in an effort to find balance in their world when one kid seems to get a slightly larger cookie than the other received. "Make it fair, mommy!"

While we may be able to balance the scales amongst children occasionally, in the adult world, there is indeed no fairness.

The universe is unconcerned with our concept of fairness. Is it fair that very few hatchling turtles ever make it to the water, and dreadfully few survive long enough to return to lay eggs themselves? Is it fair that whole forests and ecosystems go up in natural fires, displacing or killing millions of animals?

The observable truth is the universe does not contain the concept of fairness or unfairness. The universe simply is. And some argue that all the disasters big and small are perfection in that the universe continues to evolve and everything is happening exactly as it should.

We suffer because we desire that which we do not have. This is one interpretation of the four noble truths of Buddhism. We desire our world to be fair, and when it isn't then we suffer. In that suffering we are then compelled to take matters into our own hands and attempt to create justice or fairness, which is fundamentally impossible, so we suffer again at the lack of fairness. Vicious circle isn't it?

The liberation from this suffering is to give up desire. If we give up the notion that things can be truly fair, then we can be free of the burden of creating the impossible. We should continue to fight for justice but not be devastated when it doesn't happen. We should try for a balance in life, but be accepting when it proves too difficult.

My solution is to mourn the death of fairness as an absolute concept and instead try to live better in harmony, accepting that this is a random world where good and bad are unevenly distributed among the population.

I'll take responsibility for creating the best world for myself, my family, and my friends, using the talents and skills afforded to me. I'll be the architect of my own destiny. I'll shape my future and not rely on random fairness or for anyone to send me unlooked for blessings. Dang that feels good!

Flexibility of Thought

There are many people who are so convinced that their thought process is correct, they'll defend to the death their point of view. I've seen many times in my private psychology practice the habit of each individual, telling his or her story, with a fervency that inspires one to believe every word.

It is as if the listener could only experience the details of the person's story so specifically and through the teller's eyes that they too would come to the exact same conclusions and make the same choices. The problem with this strategy is that the experience is subjective rather than objective.

The teller of the story is convinced of the correctness of their observation as well as their own conclusions. They also assume that each person given the same options would choose their choice, which is very false.

This attitude can be particularly difficult to deal with in family therapy situations where the mother, father, and child all are trying to convince the therapist of their truth. Or a relationship problem where each person is indeed steadfast in their *observed truth*.

We don't allow much for the possibility that, either we did not perceive correctly or that our brain would come to an incorrect conclusion, and would not allow us to engage in an incorrect course of action. We justify our perceptions, thoughts, conclusions, and choices because it spares us the shame of a mistake.

Growth can only occur when we surrender to the idea that there are other ways of perceiving situations and other choices that can be made. Unfortunately this conclusion is far too difficult to accept for many of us humans. Simple, one-answer choices are what we're looking for. It takes a great deal of courage to be flexible in thinking. To consider that our perception is faulty, clouded, or incomplete, while painful, can lead to a greater understanding. This is especially true in social situations.

Thrivers know and accept that their observations are biased. They seek corroboration and collaboration with others to clarify experiences. This will lead them to making more accurate choices based on more information.

A wise person will seek not to be expert in every situation but to learn from others and consider other points of view. One view of enlightenment is the awareness of unlimited solutions to the same problem.

Words That Just Don't Work

There are some words and phrases that simply irk me. I get irritated when patients in my office utter them. These words bother me because they often hinder the direct flow of conversation or they are limiting in our thinking. They're excuses for not doing the work that is so important to *thriving*.

I don't know. This is a statement of laziness. Simply because the question that preceded it provokes a going inward to uncomfortableness, doesn't mean that we should use the easy escape of I don't know. A question like "why do you think that you self-sabotage?" should not be answered with "I don't know." The question was aimed to make a person *think!*

If I ask: "What is the square root of 4733?" I would expect you to do the math required to find the answer. We have become lazy in our thinking, and it's too easy to answer difficult questions with I don't know. My advice is to banish this string of words, and do the math. Dig deep and the answers you find will illuminate your subconscious mind, which allows the conscious mind to retake control of your life.

Just. Just is a minimizer, as in; I just had a couple of drinks, or I just didn't pay attention, or I was just saying... The word just softens or minimizes the original intent and that lazy way of speaking keeps us from accepting responsibility for our behaviors.

But. Yeah, but... a client of mine in group session once challenged another client speaking. They had started their defense of their addiction with the phrase, Yeah, but... and my client interrupted them with the statement: "Everything that comes after 'yeah, but...' is bullshit!" Using but in our self-dialogue is often an excuse, it should be very limited.

Because. This is also an excuse and often minimizes the situation or conditions. Should be used very sparingly.

And lastly, *can't.* Can't is a lazy word and convinces us of our own inferiority. "If you say you can or you say you can't, you are absolutely correct." Henry Ford.

CHAPTER 31

The Last Lecture, Leaving Your Legacy

"Proud of my father? I think I am proud of the legacy he left...he left us so much." **Ziggy Marley**

I recently reread *The Last Lecture*, by Randy Pausch. If you haven't read it, put this book on your mandatory read list. There is also an amazing video on Youtube that has gotten millions of hits. A wonderful explanation of what Randy learned about life in his short term on this planet.

Randy Pausch, a professor at Carnegie Mellon University in the Computer Science department was asked to be the featured speaker at a series that was called the Last Lecture. This was a forum for a professor to speak to students and the audience about what they had learned about life as if it were the last lecture they'd ever give. As it turned out, he was indeed dying of liver cancer and this would be his actual last lecture. He also took the opportunity to share as much of his collected knowledge in a book of the same name, co-written by Jeffery Zaslow. I had the profound pleasure of interviewing Mr. Zaslow on my radio show about his experiences writing the book with Randy.

In the end, Randy wished to leave a legacy for his children, because he knew he wouldn't be there to teach them as they grew up. Sometimes we believe that the point of acquiring wisdom is to make our own lives better. Certainly that can be a wonderful effect, but I feel the point is to pass on wisdom, to share what we collect and to advance our species. Each new generation does not have to reinvent the wheel. We continuously build on the previous generations' efforts. Wisdom can be assumed into the new generation.

As an example: most of us wouldn't know the first thing about the inner workings of our automobiles, trucks, and motorcycles, but we can operate them just fine (for the most part!). In life wisdom, previous generational knowledge often does not translate to the younger generation. They reject the older as outdated.

Each of us must acquire wisdom through experience but also through paying attention to the ones who have gone before. Experience is an excellent teacher, however, you will never live long enough to experience everything you need to know.

So we set about learning from our parents, teachers, coaches, and mentors about life. There's also an amazing amount of wisdom stored in media such as movies, music, poetry, and other art forms. Even historical figures can be mentors of wisdom by the legacy they leave behind. For instance, I have always admired Abraham Lincoln because of his ability to achieve despite depression and many failures.

With regards to life wisdom, each generation seems to either wish to build their knowledge through personal experience alone, or depend entirely on ancient wisdom from books and traditions going back thousands of years. Right here, right now, there is wisdom to be discovered.

Our current times demand a different kind of adaptation in order to not merely survive but to *thrive*! Balance is what's called for. Neither totally depending on the past, nor totally depending on experience.

Randy Pausch knew he was going to die. He had a defined period of time to collect all that he had learned and deemed worthy of sharing to others, especially his kids. We're all going to die. Most of us don't know when. Wouldn't it be a special gift if we could write down what we know and share it with our children and perhaps our grandchildren? Maybe our wisdom can reach across the ages to many generations.

My attempts to share what I've learned come from a place of kindness. I do not wish to jealously guard information, but rather to share with everybody what I discover to be very understandable concepts. I wish to reach the widest audience possible with messages of hope, joy, and love.

My Life is a movie, starring Michael Keaton. His character in the movie receives the news from his doctors that he is dying and will not be able to be around to teach his unborn son all that he wished to share as a father. He embarks on an odyssey to videotape (yes, the movie is that old) all the things he wanted to teach his child. Things like how to throw a football, and how to shave, or start a car with jumper cables. In the end he also teaches his son how to let go of resentments and fear.

As a father, I try to teach my son what I know. Things that will help him be a better person and how to engage life fully. As a psychologist, I need to help people find their own answers from deep inside. I show them how to take the journey. As an author, I have even more freedom to empty my skull and be a storyteller.

Whether young or old, if you haven't yet made your mark on the world, now is the time to think about what your legacy will be. As you move through life, collect the wisdom that is freely given by your mentors, through the books you choose to read, and setting yourself up for life experiences that teach that wisdom.

Be fearless and relentless in your pursuit of wisdom that you can share with the next generation. You will not get wise just by staying alive. There are many old people who are not wise. You will gain the wisdom, by looking for it, and taking it into your heart and mind.

Avoid jealously guarding your wisdom. Share it freely. Let go of the idea that you have nothing to share, let go that you are ashamed of your mistakes. Even the biggest screw up (that is how I have seen myself) have learned a few tricks.

Randy Paush knew he had a very limited time to collect, compile, and share his wisdom with his children, and through his book, also share with the rest of us. Every human has a limited time on this planet to collect, compile, and joyously share wisdom with the next generation. Share it in written work through a personal journal or write a book. Perhaps teaching others a few pieces of wisdom will do the trick. Share it on video or something that's enduring, because in sharing, one assures a certain immortality and during the creative process we thrive!

CHAPTER 32

A Good Dark Suit

"Grief is the price we pay for love." **Queen Elizabeth II**

"It is not death that a man should fear, but he should fear never beginning to live." **Marcus Aurelius**

This is the darkest chapter I have ever written. I have struggled with it for almost three years now. My struggle is because of my intent to be motivating, which then leads to an avoidance of dwelling on dark subject matter. However, when it comes to thriving, I must be honest about all of the challenges we humans must face.

Thrivers tend to grow from challenges rather than merely endure them. One of the most important life lessons I ever learned was from a 96-year-old man at an amazing party, in famous Topanga Canyon, California. The year was 1995.

This party was unique in that there were people of all ages attending and socializing freely without it being a family gathering. Most parties I had attended up to that point in my life were self-segregated by age, kids' birthday, high school cool, twenty something hip, etc. There were doctors and ditch diggers, *homies* and homemakers, musicians and accountants. The mix was rather stimulating.

I met Zeke, a tall and lean 96-year-old man who also happened to be one of the coolest dudes I ever had the pleasure to hang out with. He was vibrant, fun, full of stories, and collecting phone numbers from all the hot chicks in their 60's! After listening to some music a few of us were playing on guitars, we struck up a conversation.

I had to ask him what his secret was to a long life. I was sure he had answered that question a thousand times before and I assumed his answer would be something like; eat your vegetables, or get exercise every day, or don't worry too much. But he said something much deeper and profound. He said, "Son, get yourself a good dark suit." "What?" I asked. How would that get me to live a long life? "Son, if you want to live as long as me, then you are going to go to an awful lot of damn funerals."

What he was telling me was that the longer one lives, the likelihood of the occurrence of tragedy and death one will have to deal with increases. We cannot let it crush us. The processing of grief is a critical life skill. Not everyone currently in your life will always be there and we must find ways of processing that grief.

This lesson was most important for me. Throughout my life, I've been in the path of many deaths. My brother's suicide at twenty years old affected me so deeply that it's impossible to express in words. Many other deaths of family, friends, co-workers, and even patients of mine over the years have taken their toll on me. Remembering to understand that death is part of the cycle of life and must be dealt with, keeps me sane.

I've seen amazing growth from trauma from individuals that are aware enough to make the choice to grow. I am one of those people. Change is inevitable, growth is optional.

The idea for this book came from the question people have asked me over and over. "How do you keep rising from the ashes of tragedy again and again?" My answer is by having the *courage* to *thrive*, thus the name of this book.

Regarding Zeke's good dark suit, he was prepared to be buried in it. He was not fearful of death, as he had made peace with his life and his belief about what comes after. Having faced my own death many times, I too am ready but in no hurry. I have things to do. I don't fear death, but fear never really living a glorious life. That's another reason I am so set on thriving in this life that's available to me.

I know the sound of ultimate suffering. There are very few times in anyone's life where the shared experience of our humanity is at its most basic and crucial. These events can be life changing. Pivotal moments change the course of our lives, and in these moments we find our humanity.

I was driving to an evening martial arts class, just as dusk was shifting into night. You know the time of day, when shadows play tricks across the roadway, oncoming headlights seem a bit too bright and distracting, and depth perception is more difficult.

As traffic began to pick up speed on this particularly busy street, I began to slow because several people were running across the road in front of us, looking like a line of human sized quail running in dark silhouetted single file. At the same time, a motorcycle behind me raced past, obviously annoyed at the slow down. What happened next unfolded in horrifying slow motion, and will forever be burned into my brain.

The speeding, reckless motorcycle, in the full spotlight of my headlights, hit the last person in the line running across the street. He hit this person with such force, their shoes were left in place in the roadway. The motorcyclist careened to the side of the road where he smashed into the back end of a parked car. Traffic screeching to a halt, I jumped from my truck to rush to the impact scene.

What lay before me was a woman who was covered in blood and almost unrecognizable as human because of her injuries. My instinct was to check for a pulse but it was no use. I held her as she took her agonizing last breaths. Somehow I knew that I had to stay with her in these moments to comfort her. It was then that I heard that unmistakable sound of ultimate suffering.

A man, who I assumed was the woman's husband was on his knees, wailing on the side of the road. He must have been realizing what had just happened, and who this horribly mangled person was in the middle of the road. All he could do was wail. It was deep and throbbing, without any ability to be consoled. I never spoke to him. What words could I possibly say?

The police and ambulances arrived. The business of investigation was conducted. My account was written down. I later learned that the motorcyclist had been three times over the legal limit for alcohol; they found him guilty of vehicular manslaughter.

I returned home covered in blood and in a state of shock. Processing what I had seen and experienced took quite some time. Because of my experiences in my personal therapy, I had some tools to deal with my feelings. And in the end, what made sense to me was that for some reason, I needed to be there to provide comfort to that poor woman, if even for just a few moments.

Since that time, I have been exposed to many more deaths, but with a new focus. My ability to be human, compassionate, and comforting drives me to stay with the uncomfortable feelings and stay with people near the end of life. We are all here for a short time, some shorter than others. But we must accept the truth that death is a part of our human experience. Running away from that reality will hurt far more that facing the truth.

How can I thrive when others have lost their lives? How can I thrive when people I love have met with their final end? It seems so unfair. But I know that I must thrive to give honor to those who are no longer here. It's by thriving that I give respect to their human experience. I too shall die one day, and I expect all those who are still living, to indeed go on thriving.

The solutions to working through grief, trauma, and loss are many and varied. Some find solace in religion, some find that the processing with a therapist to be very helpful, and still others can work through it with the help of supportive friends and relatives. There is no correct or right way. If grief, trauma, or loss is holding you back from a thriving life, then you must embark on a journey of healing in order reconcile the dark feelings and drain the residual stored energy that causes the pain.

Dr. Gabor Mate reminds us of the wisdom of the *Tibetan Book of Living and Dying*. "Whatever you do, don't try to escape from your pain but be with it." He also states, "A person can only be with their pain in the presence of compassion." Therefore, the solution is to seek out a compassionate present in the form of friends, family, clergy, and therapists. Most of all, we have to find inner peace and be compassionate with ourselves.

Zeke was correct. Own a good dark suit, or whatever clothes give respect to the solemnity of a funeral. Additionally, we need to develop mechanisms of self-soothing and caring for others with compassion and love. Together we comfort each other and share the chance to continue thriving. We can do nothing for life that is lost, except give honor by thriving with the life we have left.

CHAPTER 33

Why do I Ride?

> "At the end of a long day on the road, I felt the mixed buzz of all-day vibration, over stimulation, and weariness—a refrain that often played in my head: When I'm riding my motorcycle, I'm glad to be alive. When I stop riding my motorcycle, I'm glad to be alive." **Neal Peart**

Many people ask me why I ride a motorcycle. I have ridden for so long that people expect me to show up on one of my bikes, and I am often referred to as *The Psych on the Bike*. It didn't seem to be the obvious choice for me as I was such an awkward teenager. I once tripped over a single brick in an empty room!

A father and family man should drive a sensible vehicle like a car or SUV, shouldn't he? Riding a bike is dangerous. And my carelessness in youth nearly cost me my life. In my wilder, younger days, I was in a few motorcycle mishaps and even shut down a freeway with a spectacular crash. But nothing has prevented me from climbing back in the saddle.

Why the obsession with the open road? There is no other question that sparks such varied responses among motorcycle riders. For most of us, it is an intangible feeling of being alive. More alive than when we are just walking around or driving a car. For me, it really is a celebration of being alive. It represents the freedom to live fully. It gives me the opportunity to really thrive in life, and not just get to the next location. The wind in my face seems to blow my cares away. For me it's therapy.

Several times now I have taken my son, Devin, on long road trips throughout California on our sidecar motorcycle rig. We meet up with amazing people, explore the sights, and share invaluable father/son bonding experiences. Many times along the road, I find myself visually drinking in the spectacular natural beauty and to do this with my son is a tremendous pleasure.

From acres of rolling hills covered in grape vines and wineries, to the fields filled with emerald green grass and wild flowers, to the stunning shoreline, and along the deep forest roads, we are enveloped in an experience that is better than any 3D movie. We share these experiences, and they'll forever be a part of our relationship.

Most of the miles I ride each year are alone on my daily commute to the treatment center in Malibu, and my private practice office to see clients. Riding a motorcycle requires an intense focus that surprisingly, is not draining, but in fact rather liberating. It requires the rider to anticipate the future, looking ahead in the road not just at the road underneath.

Riding to me is a moving meditation. I listen to the engine, watch the conditions of the road, shift through the gears, blending myself with the machine and motion. Nothing compares to riding home in the evening as the wind blows away my stress leaving me refreshed as I arrive to my family.

For me it's about living an inspired life. I got that phrase from motivational speaker and radio personality, Susan Burrell. She really is on to something here; that we should strive to live fully and completely, without reservations. Check out her website at www.livingyourinspiredlife.org.

Motorcycling, for me is a part of living an inspired life. It also is not allowing past mistakes to define my existence. I learn from my mistakes and grow. This is the essence of thriving. If we always avoid situations that caused pain or discomfort, then our world will be constantly shrinking until we are frozen with fear.

I have also taken long solo rides, which allow me to spend time in my head and just think uninterrupted. Most people when driving their car need the distraction or entertainment of the radio. Sometimes it really is better to not listen to the news. I cannot tell you how pleasurable it is to not listen to talk radio with all their anger and vitriol. My mind can become clear and free when I ride.

A favorite ride of mine is up the California coast solo, then somewhere up near Monterey to connect with my soul brother, Will Carter. A couple of years ago he and I met up in San Jose and rode down the coast together. Gliding effortlessly through the giant redwoods of Big Sur and along the craggy yet beautiful coastline of central California. Each time we stopped we would talk about what we'd seen along the road. Then in the evening at a restaurant, we would philosophize on life, just two comrades enjoying the moments. These shared experiences bring richness to our existence.

In the book, *Zen and the Art of Motorcycle Maintenance*, Rober Pirsig regales us with the inner musings of his mind on a cross-country trip with his son. He explains beautifully the musical accompaniment of the mechanics of his engine, listening to the valves and exhaust notes while pondering the meaning of the word *quality*.

There is indeed a Zen mentality that envelops a rider, as the wind brushes his cheeks and the road zips underneath. We are soothed by the vibrations of the engine and the road. Sure there is danger, but the thrill and the achievement of The Zen mind achieved is worth it.

Neil Peart, the drummer for the progressive rock band Rush, wrote a book of his travels by motorcycle called *Ghost Rider, Travels on the Healing Road*. His journey of over 55,000 miles began when he suffered the tragic loss of his daughter to a car accident, then ten months later, his wife to cancer. On the road, he processes his grief and finds the will to live. He finds meaning in his life and eventually, once again, love. On a motorcycle there is time to think.

Thriving is about facing fear head on. Not being stupid about fear, but refusing to let fear rule our lives. When I was young and self-destructive, I took my love of motorcycling for granted and behaved badly. As I mature, I've learned to find the deeper meaning in each of my choices and to live fully, in each moment. Embracing my persona as the *Psych on the Bike*, I will live what I teach and represent the courage to thrive every day.

What is your courageous act? What are you going to do to face your fears? How will you endeavor to *thrive*?

Epilogue

After reading this chapter, I was cruising down the Southern California canyons, enjoying the sights and smells of the early morning. It occurred to me that there are more reasons beyond the esoteric, philosophical, and psychological reasons for my love of riding are some other more visceral reasons for why I ride.

Firstly, the fresh air is just delightful. I really cannot stand the stuffiness of being in a car. Even with the air conditioner on, the air just seems stale. On a bike, the air is moving, wind in the face, smile on my face!

Secondly, the smells of nature are ever present. I am indeed fortunate to live and ride in such beautiful country and not battling it out in city traffic. The smells of the various native sages, pines, oaks, laurels, and brickellbush are simply intoxicating at times.

Thirdly, the feeling of leaning into the turns. It is so hard to describe the kinesthetic value of the lean. Carving through the *twisties* is an experience that just has to be felt, in order to be understood. Suffice it to say, that it insists that you are alive and an active participant in the driving experience.

And lastly, the roar of the engine. That deep throaty growl as I roll on the throttle, coming out of a turn vibrates through the entire body. That whole body reward as I connect to the machine is just about the best feeling ever. The vibration is my evidence of thriving. That is why I ride.

CHAPTER 34

Gift of Life

"Love is a sacred reserve of energy; it is like the blood of spiritual evolution."
Pierre Teilhard de Chardin

Blood. I've spilled a lot of it over my lifetime. Skinned knees, cut fingers, bloody noses, bicycle accidents, car accidents, motorcycle accidents, cut bare feet, fist fights, fell off a telephone pole, four surgeries, rose thorns, split lip, even a friendly rock fight as a kid that left a really nice scar on my head (it's another story)! But I am most proud of the blood I have spilled by donation to the Red Cross and our local hospital.

My son, Devin, was born three months premature in 1999. Back then, I was in graduate school and felt that I was giving everything I had to keep my life together. With a sick child in intensive care, I was struggling to keep my head above water. School, work, home, and child in hospital all conspired to rob me of nearly every ounce of energy.

One day, my son's doctor asked me what blood type I was. "O positive, but why?" I answered. He asked if I would be willing to give blood as a *directed donation* to Devin, in need of an immediate blood transfusion. YES! Anything I could, I would do for him. So right then and there I donated blood for the first time.

Since that time, I have donated on average three times a year. I was so proud when they gave me a 1 gallon pin. Eight pints was a cool milestone. It meant that I have been able to help many, people.

Most of my donations have gone to anonymous people but occasionally, I have the privilege to do a directed donation. A couple of years ago, I received an email asking for blood donations for a little girl with leukemia. She was nine months old and needed weekly blood transfusions until she could get a bone marrow transplant.

My blood is what they call CMV negative. This means that I have never been exposed to the Cytomegalovirus, and can donate to premature infants, and babies. 60% of people age 6 or older have been exposed and by age 80 it is over 90%. Even the anti-bodies are found to have negative or even fatal effects for premature infants. I donated twice to this little girl and eventually a bone marrow donor was found. She is now doing wonderfully and living well.

When I gave to my son, love was the reason. When I give again, it will continue to be with love. By giving precious, lifesaving blood, my life has been elevated each time. Acts of altruism reward the individual so profoundly and dramatically because it is actually taking what is within, and then putting it out to help others. Giving to others is love. Love is the blood of spiritual evolution. It is a catalyst for change.

Having donated to specific people and had a helping part in saving their lives is one of the greatest feelings ever. The giving of oneself without any expectation of reward, takes us to a higher plane of existence. In that moment we *thrive*!

I highly encourage you to give if you can. And if for some reason you are not a good candidate to donate, then find a way of getting involved somehow. Volunteer, donate money, do something that helps others.

One of the most important concepts in the courage to thrive is finding the reason to act. An action can come from one of four motivations. 1: reward. 2: punishment. 3: self-mastery. 4: altruism. The first two, reward and punishment, are extrinsically motivated. One is avoiding some form of punishment or pain, or one is seeking a reward. It is how we motivate children and puppy dogs. But the latter two, self-mastery and altruism, are intrinsically motivating.

The most mature, deepest meaning, and profoundly personal impact comes from being selfless. I have expanded on this concept in the chapter on the Four Reasons. Altruism is love.

January is national blood donor month. To give the gift of life is about the most selfless thing you can do. The courage to thrive means that you have so much to give, you cannot keep it to yourself. Your body is capable of producing extra blood. When you donate, your bone marrow and other systems engage to replace the lost components, plasma, platelets, and red blood cells. One pint of donated blood can save 3 lives! Please give blood. Save lives and *thrive*! And they give you free cookies.

To make an appointment to schedule a donation contact; American Red Cross http://www.redcrossblood.org/, or contact your local hospital.

Conclusion

"Courage is not the absence of fear; courage is what we do in the presence of fear." **Dr. Stephen Trudeau**

This journey of exploration has had a singular goal, to inspire you to truly *thrive*! Too much of our lives have been spent in the victim mentality, utilizing maladaptive strategies to just get by or barely survive. In surviving we are simply waiting for the next insult, trauma, or tragedy to knock us down, living lives of quiet desperation.

We are meant thrive, not just get by. Life is an amazing adventure, filled with awesome experiences. Peak moments that fill us with joy, happiness, and love. This is what we should strive for. To thrive is to grow.

Childhood trauma and/or the collection of simple life insults leave us vulnerable wounded. It is only natural to want to protect ourselves, however, the maladaptive strategies hold us back and have devastating side effects.

The better strategy is to muster our courage, step out of the comfort zone, and embrace the strategies that will allow us to truly thrive! Thriving is a way of life. It's deliberate living and being the architect of our own destiny rather than being a victim waiting for life to just happen.

We defend our poor choices, our self-limiting choices by acknowledging the fear, the pain, and the discomfort of difficult actions. This strategy has led to us living lives that are diminished and small.

Thrivers have taken the time to discover their *core self* and are committed to personal growth. They most importantly acquire the skills to adapt to the ever-changing needs of their environment. And they believe they can shape their future. This is *thriving*. Rising from the ashes, like the fabled Phoenix, over and over, becoming stronger and more beautiful with each challenge.

The love we seek can only be experienced internally. In order to have access to that internal feeling, we need to find a way to love ourselves. All the techniques and strategies in the world will not make a difference if we do not apply them. We have to love ourselves enough to take the chance and try something new. When we live with an abundance of love, we then have enough left over to share with the world.

In order to truly thrive, we must have the courage to take action and live deliberately. It's time for you to apply these principle and live the life you have always imagined you could live. I believe in you. I expect you to *thrive!*